DAY WALKS IN THE DOLOMITES

50 SHORT WALKS AND ALL-DAY HIKES IN THE ITALIAN DOLOMITES

by Gillian Price

JUNIPER HOUSE, MURLEY MOSS,
OXENHOLME ROAD, KENDAL, CUMBRIA LA9 7RL
www.cicerone.co.uk

© Gillian Price 2023
Fourth edition 2023
ISBN: 978 1 78631 121 4
Reprinted 2024 (with updates)
First edition 2002
Printed in Czechia on behalf of Latitude Press Ltd on responsibly sourced paper.
A catalogue record for this book is available from the British Library.

MIX
Paper | Supporting
responsible forestry
FSC® C014138
www.fsc.org

Route mapping by Lovell Johns www.lovelljohns.com
All photographs are by the author unless otherwise stated.
Contains OpenStreetMap.org data © OpenStreetMap
contributors, CC-BY-SA. NASA relief data courtesy of ESRI

Acknowledgements

As usual, Nicola was the perfect companion.

Updates to this guide

While every effort is made by our authors to ensure the accuracy of guidebooks as they go to print, changes can occur during the lifetime of an edition. Any updates that we know of for this guide will be on the Cicerone website (www.cicerone.co.uk/1121/updates), so please check before planning your trip. We also advise that you check information about such things as transport, accommodation and shops locally. Even rights of way can be altered over time. We are always grateful for information about any discrepancies between a guidebook and the facts on the ground, sent by email to updates@cicerone.co.uk.

Register your book: To sign up to receive free updates, special offers and GPX files where available, create a Cicerone account and register your purchase via the 'My Account' tab at www.cicerone.co.uk.

Note on mapping

The route maps in this guide are derived from publicly available data, databases and crowd-sourced data. As such they have not been through the detailed checking procedures that would generally be applied to a published map from an official mapping agency. However, we have reviewed them closely in the light of local knowledge as part of the preparation of this guide.

Front cover: Walkers en route to Passo Principe, in the Catinaccio (Walk 37)

CONTENTS

Mountain safety

Every mountain walk has its dangers, and those described in this guidebook are no exception. All who walk or climb in the mountains should recognise this and take responsibility for themselves and their companions along the way. The author and publisher have made every effort to ensure that the information contained in this guide was correct when it went to press, but, except for any liability that cannot be excluded by law, they cannot accept responsibility for any loss, injury or inconvenience sustained by any person using this book.

International distress signal *(emergency only)*
Six blasts on a whistle (and flashes with a torch after dark) spaced evenly for one minute, followed by a minute's pause. Repeat until an answer is received. The response is three signals per minute followed by a minute's pause.

Helicopter rescue
The following signals are used to communicate with a helicopter:

Help needed:
raise both arms
above head to
form a 'Y'

Help not needed:
raise one arm
above head, extend
other arm downward

Emergency telephone numbers
General emergency tel 112
Soccorso alpino (mountain rescue) tel 118

Weather reports
Trentino *www.meteotrentino.it*
Veneto *www.arpa.veneto.it*
Weather South Tyrol (app also available) *https://weather.provinz.bz.it*

Mountain rescue can be very expensive – be adequately insured.

Symbols used on route maps

～	route	🍴	meals/refreshments
＿＿	alternative route	◉	bus stop
Ⓢ	start point	🅿	car park
Ⓕ	finish point	𝒊	tourist information
ⓈⒻ	start/finish point	✳	viewpoint
ⓈⒻ	alternative start/finish	·	other feature
➤	route direction		
	glacier		
	woodland		
	urban areas		
	international border		
⬛	funicular		
▪	station/railway		
▲	peak		
⌂	refuge with accommodation		
⌂	other accommodation/hotel		
⌂	bivouac hut		
▪	building		
†	cross/church/chapel		
🏰	castle		
⌣	pass		
=	bridge		
🚡	cable car		
🚠	gondala		
🚡	chairlift		

Relief
in metres

3400–3600
3200–3400
3000–3200
2800–3000
2600–2800
2400–2600
2200–2400
2000–2200
1800–2000
1600–1800
1400–1600
1200–1400
1000–1200
800–1000
600–800
400–600
200–400
0–200

SCALE: 1:50,000

0 kilometres 0.5   1

0 miles   0.5

Contour lines are drawn at 25m intervals and highlighted at 100m intervals.

Maps are drawn at 1:50,000 unless otherwise stated.

GPX files for all routes can be downloaded free at www.cicerone.co.uk/1121/GPX.

Cosy Rifugio Pertini (Walk 40)

ROUTE SUMMARY TABLE

Walk	Title	Start/Finish	Distance	Ascent/Descent	Grade	Time	Page
1	Lago di Braies	Hotel Lago di Braies	3.5km	50m	1	1hr 30	44
2	Rifugio Biella Loop	Hotel Lago di Braies	16km	950m	2	5hr 50	47
3	Monte Specie	Pratopiazza	8km	340m	1–2	2hr 45	51
4	Alpe di Sennes Circuit	Rifugio Malga Ra Stua	17km	830m	1–2	5hr 15	54
5	Landro to Cortina on the Old Railway Line	Gasthof Drei Zinnen/Cortina d'Ampezzo	20km	120m/350m	1	4hr 30	59
6	Torre dei Scarperi Circuit	Antoniusstein car park, Val Campo di Dentro	13.5km	1019m	2	5hr 30	65
7	The Val Fiscalina Tour	Dolomitenhof, Pian di Val Fiscalina	17.8km	1225m	2	6hr	68
8	The Tre Cime di Lavaredo Loop	Rifugio Auronzo	9.8km	450m	1–2	3hr 30	73
9	Through the Cadini di Misurina	Lago d'Antorno	8.5km	580m	2+	3hr 10	78
10	Monte Piana	Lago d'Antorno (or Bar Genzianella for jeep shuttle)	14km	920m	2+	4hr 30	82
11	Lago di Misurina	Grand Hotel Misurina bus stop	3km	-	1	1hr	86
12	Val Popena Alta	Misurina tourist office	7km	600m	2–3	2hr 30	89
13	Rifugio Vandelli Traverse	Passo Tre Croci	12.5km	800m	2–3	5hr	92

Walk	Title	Start/Finish	Distance	Ascent/Descent	Grade	Time	Page
14	Forcella Zumèles and the Cristallo	Rio Gere	9.6km	550m	2+	3hr 15	96
15	Below the Antelao	*Centro* bus stop, San Vito di Cadore	17.5km	1200m	2	5hr 30	99
16	Rifugio Padova and Rifugio Tita Barba	Car park near Rifugio Padova	12km	950m	2	5hr 15	103
17	The Pramper Circuit	Pian de la Fopa, Val Pramper	13.5km	750m	1–2	4hr 15	106
18	Lago Coldai and the Civetta	Alleghe gondola lifts/Listolade	20.5km	800m/2040m	2	7hr	109
19	The Pelmo Tour	Passo Staulanza	13.5km	1100m	3	6hr	115
20	Gores de Federa	Campo di Sotto, Cortina	15km	770m	2	4hr	119
21	Around the Croda da Lago	Ponte di Rocurto	13.5km	950m	2+	5hr	122
22	The Cinque Torri	Bai de Dones chairlift	7.5km	400m	2	3hr 30	126
23	Up the Nuvolau	Rifugio Col Gallina	9.6km	700m	2	4hr 10	129
24	Skirting the Tofana di Rozes	Da Strobel car park, near Passo Falzarego	13km	800m	2	4hr 45	133
25	The Lagazuoi Tunnels	Passo Falzarego	6km	600m	3	3hr 15	137
26	The Kaiserjäger Route	Passo di Valparola	9.5km	700m	2–3	4hr	140
27	Round the Settsass	Passo di Valparola	13km	950m	2	5hr 30	144

Walk	Title	Start/Finish	Distance	Ascent/Descent	Grade	Time	Page
28	Santa Croce Sanctuary	Badia/Pedraces chair lift/bus stop	9.5km	100m/650m	1–2	3hr 15	149
29	Sass de Putia	Passo delle Erbe	17.5km	1100m	2–3	6hr	153
30	Sentiero delle Odle	Ranui, upper Val di Funes	17km	950m	2	5hr	158
31	The Rasciesa Ridge	Main square, Ortisei	17.5km	280m/900m	1–2	4hr 45	162
32	Across the Puez-Odle Altopiano	Dantercepies gondola lift station, Selva di Val Gardena	16km	500m/1150m	2	5hr	167
33	The Bullaccia Tour	Gondola lift arrival station, Compaccio	8.8km	380m	1	3hr	172
34	Alpe di Siusi Circuit and Rifugio Bolzano	Tourist Office, Compaccio	11.5km	500m	2	3hr 10	175
35	Castel Presule	Tourist Office, Fiè	7.5km	325m	1	2hr 20	179
36	Val Ciamin	Bus stop, San Cipriano	11km	570m	1–2	4hr	183
37	The Inner Catinaccio	Rifugio Ciampedie	12.5km	810m	3	5hr	187
38	Sentiero del Masaré	Passo di Costalunga/Malga Frommer	12.2km	670m	2	4hr 20	192
39	The Latemar Labyrinth and Lago di Carezza	Grand Hotel Carezza	10.8km	400m	1–2	3hr	195
40	Circumnavigating Sassopiatto-Sassolungo	Passo Sella	16.5km	850m	2	6hr	200
41	The Sella and Piz Boè	Passo Pordoi cable-car station	8km	560m	2–3	3hr 15	205

Walk	Title	Start/Finish	Distance	Ascent/Descent	Grade	Time	Page
42	Viel del Pan	Passo Pordoi/Arabba	6.5km	380m/150m	1–2	2hr 20	209
43	The Sas de Adam Crest	Ciampac gondola lift/Pozza di Fassa	8km	350m/450m	2	3hr	213
44	The Marmolada and Punta Serauta	Malga Ciapela cable car	2.5km	150m	2	1hr 30	218
45	Rifugio Falier in Valle Ombretta	Malga Ciapela	12.5km	650m	1–2	3hr 40	221
46	Rifugio Mulaz	Baita Segantini	12.5km	900m	2	4hr 50	226
47	The Pale di San Martino Altopiano	Col Verde gondola lift, San Martino di Castrozza	12km	780m	2–3	5hr 20	229
48	Val Canali and Rifugio Treviso	Rifugio Cant del Gal, Val Canali	8km	550m	2	3hr 40	234
49	The Brenta Dolomites Tour	Groste gondola lift/Vallesinella	13km	220m/1140m	2	5hr 10	237
50	Val d'Ambiez	Rifugio al Cacciatore	5.7km	600m	1–2	2hr 20	241

The descent from Rifugio Tuckett e Sella (Walk 49)

PREFACE

It's been an especially 'hard' couple of years working on this new edition. Revisiting walks, collating notes about changed conditions and refuges, researching and exploring new routes, taking more photos, and then having to make the awfully difficult decision about whether to ditch an existing walk to make room for a new entry. Agony! But what a privilege to be able to pop up to these beautiful mountains for 'work'. Hope you appreciate the new material. Makes you want to go walking in the Dolomites, doesn't it?

UNESCO added the Dolomites to its World Heritage list in 2009 and visitor numbers have soared as the world flocks here in admiration. Now it is even more important to emphasise more responsible management helped by environment-conscious walkers to ensure this paradise can be enjoyed by future generations. This guide actively encourages the use of public transport – it's definitely doable; I don't have a car.

Gillian Price, Venice, January 2023

The rather steep scree route up to Forcella d'Arcia (Walk 19)

INTRODUCTION

During the final descent of Walk 38, you look back up to Rifugio Fronza beneath the Coronelle

THE DOLOMITES

A traveller who has visited all the other mountain-regions of Europe, and remains ignorant of the scenery of the Dolomite Alps, has yet to make acquaintance with Nature in one of her loveliest and most fascinating aspects.

John Ball, Guide to the Eastern Alps (1868)

Like the Alps to which they belong, the astounding Dolomite mountains in northeast Italy were long regarded with awe by the herders and woodcutters who lived around their bases. It was not until the 1800s and the advent of 'travelling', that the first leisure-seeking visitors ventured in the steps of hunters through treacherous passes to marvel at the spectacular scenery and brilliant sunsets. Published accounts and guidebooks began to appear, and soon tourists and mountaineers from all over Europe flocked to explore the magnificence.

Nowadays, the fantastic Dolomites are an exciting and prime holiday destination in both summer and winter. Superbly located resorts are connected by excellent public transport and well-maintained roads, while an ultra-modern system of cable cars and lifts whisks visitors to dizzy heights in a matter of minutes. Nature lovers will be delighted by the fascinating wildlife in the magnificent forest and high-altitude rockscapes, along with sweet alpine meadows that summer transforms into oceans of wild flowers straight out of *The Sound of Music*. High above are breathtakingly sheer bastions and spires of delicately pale rock in an enthralling succession of bizarre sculpted shapes. The Dolomites are a collection of unique massifs which visitors will quickly learn to recognise: the throne-like Pelmo, fortress Sella, the elegant Odle needles, trident points of Tre Cime di Lavaredo and the pyramidal Antelao are but a few. Visitors have plenty of magnificence to look forward to.

They can easily be appreciated thanks to the great network of signed paths that snake over ridges and valleys linking welcoming refuges, where meals and refreshments can be enjoyed with a beautiful alpine backdrop thrown in for free.

This guidebook offers a selection of 50 exciting walks suitable for enthusiastic walkers of all ages, abilities and energy. There is something for everyone. The carefully graded routes range from a leisurely 2.5km stroll to a strenuous 20.5km outing for experienced walkers via panoramic peaks. Each walk has been designed to fit into a single day. This means you don't need to carry a huge rucksack and can return to comfortable accommodation at day's end.

LONGER WALKS AND TREKS

For more ambitious walkers and trekkers, 25 multiple-day routes are detailed in the Cicerone guide *Walking in the Dolomites*, while the twin volumes *Alta Via 1 – Trekking in the Dolomites* and *Alta Via 2 – Trekking in the Dolomites with AV3–6* describe six amazing long-distance routes.

WORLD WAR 1

In May 1915 on invitation from the Allies – with the promise of adding South Tyrol and Trieste to its territory – Italy entered World War 1. Due to their location, the northern Dolomites were transformed into a terrible war zone that saw the crumbling Hapsburg Empire try and defend its borders from the fledgling Italian nation. Hard-fought battles took place on mountain passes, along impossible crests and even summits. Tunnels were excavated through both cliffs and glaciers and barracks erected wherever there was a chance of shelter. More soldiers lost their lives from harsh cold and avalanches than through combat. A number of the old military supply tracks built for mules are still walkable and wartime trenches and fortifications are often encountered on the walks in this guidebook. Poignant reminders of man's folly, many have been restored thanks to EU funding.

VALLEYS AND BASES

While the Dolomites are quite compact, their geography and spiderweb of valleys can make orientation puzzling. This overview aims to help visitors find their way around and choose handy bases.

On the northernmost edge of the Dolomites is broad **Val Pusteria**. Running east–west, it acts as a low-key thoroughfare for rail and road traffic between Italy's major Isarco-Adige valley and Austria. Towards the eastern end, **Valle di Braies** branches off to enchanting **Lago di Braies**. Served by year-round bus, it has plenty of accommodation including a glorious historic hotel, café-restaurants and a plethora of memorable picnic spots. Walks 1 and 2 start out from the lake. A valley branch climbs south to the marvellous uplands of **Pratopiazza** with a hotel and refuges. Accessible by summer buses, it is perfect for Walk 3.

To the immediate east lie the spectacular Sesto Dolomites. The well-served picturesque towns of **San Candido** (trains and buses) and **Sesto** (buses) make good bases for forays into this group, and they have a full range of amenities. Walks 6 and 7 begin their exploration here.

The southern realms of the Sesto group can be accessed from Misurina, a small-scale resort with summer bus services, a scattering of guesthouses and cafés, and a campsite. It stands on the shores of a much-photographed lake, and has plenty to keep walkers busy for days as Walks 8–12 begin close by. A short bus ride away

The twin-peaked Cristallo admired from the descent route (Walk 13)

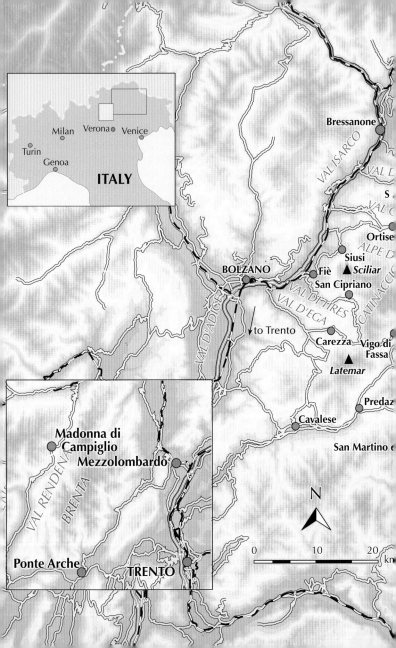

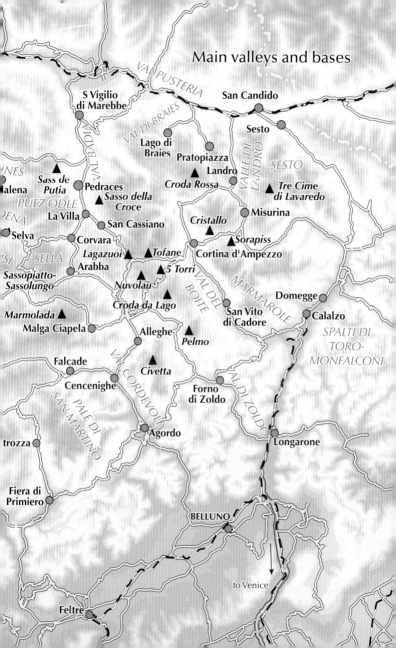

Main valleys and bases

southwest is Passo Tre Croci and the start of Walk 13 to the Sorapiss and its renowned lake. Just over the pass the towering Cristallo group can be admired on Walk 14.

Branching north from Misurina, you come to the Valle di Landro at Carbonin. A short distance away is a small lake at **Landro**, with its café, bus stop and hotel, where Walk 5 begins its delightful wander along the former Dobbiaco-Cortina railway line. After the watershed at Cimabanche, is the Walk 4 Ra Stua turn-off.

Located at an intersection of roads leading in from Dolomite passes, attractive and trendy **Cortina d'Ampezzo** is an excellent base for a couple of nights (Walks 20 and 21), although it can get rather busy (not to mention pricey). It has shops galore, hotels and year-round bus links as well as summer time runs to Passo Falzarego and Passo di Valparola, with guesthouses and cafés. In the vicinity of the passes Walks 22–27 lead around the famous Cinque Torri, Nuvolau, Tofane, Lagazuoi and neighbours.

From Cortina the scenic Val del Boite leads southeast via **San Vito di Cadore** dwarfed by the Antelao, the star of Walk 15. It is the southern-most outlier of the rugged Marmarole range which extends for 17km, a record for the Dolomites. Further on is Pieve di Cadore, the birthplace of Renaissance artist Titian, then the rail-head of Calalzo, close to **Domegge** where Walk 16 heads into the Spalti di Toro-Monfalconi.

From Pieve di Cadore, the Piave river valley heads south to **Longarone**, sadly renowned site of the 1963 Vajont dam tragedy. The Val di Zoldo (aka Valzoldano) branches northwest here, climbing past a string of quiet, hospitable villages in the shadow of the magnificent giants the Pelmo and the Civetta. The valley was an important iron-making centre in late medieval times, as place names such as Forno (furnace) and Fusine (forge) testify. Its exported nails were in great demand for shoes and shipbuilding, especially in Venice. **Forno di Zoldo** (hotels, groceries, bus) is the gateway for Walk 17, a foray into the Pramperet group, while Passo Staulanza (guest-house, summer bus) at the valley head is the start of Walk 19 around the mas-sive Pelmo.

Running almost parallel to Val di Zoldo is the **Val Cordevole** river val-ley, named for *cordubium* (dubious heart) for the fear its violent currents and waves induced in those forced to cross it. It links rail-bus transport hub Belluno via Cencenighe to relaxed **Alleghe** at the foot of the majestic Civetta. This small lakeside village offers buses, shops and accommoda-tion as well as the cable car and lifts used in Walk 18. The name comes from the Ladin *a l'ega* (on the water).

Further along, at Caprile, is a fork west for the modest resort of **Malga Ciapela** (bus, hotel, shops), where Walk 44 sets off by cable car to the dizzy heights of the 3343m glaciated Marmolada, the loftiest mountain

Walkers are dwarfed by the Civetta's western face (Walk 18)

in the Dolomites; Walk 45 passes below its south face visiting farms and refuges.

Not far away due south is the sprawling, spectacular Pale di San Martino group, easily reached from the railhead of **Feltre** thanks to year-round buses. Useful towns are **Fiera di Primiero** (accommodation, shops), for Walk 48, and **San Martino di Castrozza** (hotels, shops and lifts), for Walk 47. Higher up is Passo Rolle (places to stay and eat), for Walk 46. The road continues in descent to Paneveggio and its famed forest whose spruce once furnished wood for crafting string instruments, as well as much-needed timber for the Venetian Republic.

To the north of the Marmolada is the village of **Arabba**, where a road used by summer buses zigzags west to Passo Pordoi for hotels and cafés. Popular Walk 42 along the Viel del Pan starts off here, while Walk 41 rides the cable car to venture onto the superb, desolate, Sella massif.

From Arabba the road winds north through Passo di Campolungo to the start of beautiful Val Badia, the heart of the Ladin-language district. It is justifiably popular and rather busy at times. **Corvara**, **Badia/Pedraces** and **San Cassiano** are handy bases with a huge choice of accommodation, good bus links and plenty of shops. Walk 28 to Sasso della Croce starts at Badia/Pedraces. The valley's eastern branch climbs to Passo di Valparola – see above.

At San Martino, towards the northern extremity of Val Badia, is the steep road west for Passo delle Erbe (hotel, café, summer bus) and Walk 29 around belvedere Sass de Putia, the northernmost Dolomite. A minor road continues down to marvellous **Val di Funes** and off-the-beaten-track **Santa Maddalena** (bus, accommodation, shops). This is the jump-off for Walk 30 which wanders along the foot of the beautiful Odle rock needles.

Val di Funes is bordered by the Rasciesa ridge which separates it from **Val Gardena**, its neighbour to the south. This renowned valley, accessible by bus from Bolzano, is dotted with bustling resort villages. Lovely **Ortisei**, **Santa Cristina** and smaller **Selva** are perfect places for a base as they have accommodation, shops and year-round buses, and are handy for scenic ridge route Walk 31 as well as Walk 32, an exciting foray onto the Puez plateau. Ortisei is also famous as the birthplace of Luis Trenker, the renowned mountaineer, actor and film-maker extraordinaire from the 1930s.

Linked with Val Gardena, and also easy to reach from Bolzano, is the extensive Alpe di Siusi upland, dominated by the Sciliar massif. Handy for Walks 33 and 34 is either the lower village of **Siusi** or the upper resort of **Compaccio**. On the other hand, at the mountain foot is the photogenic village of **Fiè** (year-round bus, hotels, shops), the start for Walk 35, which wanders over meadows to a fascinating castle.

A short distance south, quiet pastoral **Val di Tires** branches off Val d'Isarco and climbs steeply towards the majestic Catinaccio, an unparalleled backdrop with its line-up of weird and wonderful rock towers and needle-like points. The valley concludes as Val Ciamin, explored in Walk 36 which begins at **San Cipriano** (accommodation, year-round buses). Then, flanked by a modern cable car, the road zigzags up towards Passo Costalunga (hotels, summer bus), a suitable base for Walk 38 (you can also get here by road and bus from Bolzano via Nova Levante). Slightly lower down is renowned pretty Lago di Carezza, visited on Walk 39. Tourism discovered this area in the mid-1850s, when ingenious engineers cut a road through the dramatic red porphyry gorge Val d'Ega, to create a link with Bolzano.

From Passo di Costalunga the road continues northeast down to Val di Fassa and Vigo di Fassa (year-round buses, hotels, shops) with its cable car into the inner Catinaccio for Walk 37. A short bus ride north is Alba and lift access for Walk 43, while further up at Passo Sella, Walk 40 embarks on its exciting circumnavigation of the Sassopiatto-Sassolungo. Popular Val di Fassa has plenty of visitor services and year-round bus runs from the city of Trento and the main railway line down in Val d'Adige.

From Trento year-round buses head west to Ponte Arche and access for Walk 50 on the southern flanks of

Rifugio Re Alberto at the foot of the superb Torri del Vaiolet (Walk 37)

the spectacular Brenta Dolomites. The road continues via Tione before veering north along **Val Rendena** to the world famous ski resort of Madonna di Campiglio. It lies at the base of the Brenta's western flanks, and offers straightforward access to mountain paths and climbing routes thanks to well-placed lifts. Along with buses, plenty of accommodation and everything else, there is a gondola lift here for Walk 49.

LANGUAGES AND PLACE NAMES

The Dolomite valleys are inhabited by speakers from three main language groups: German, Italian and Ladin. In the Südtirol, aka the South Tyrol (accounting for the north-western Dolomites), the majority (80 per cent) speak German as their mother tongue. This region belonged to the Austro-Hungarian Empire until 1918, when it was transferred to Italy after World War 1. During the advent of Fascism in the 1920s and 30s, Italian nomenclature was zealously applied to everything, with the resulting names more often than not worlds away from the original – the Südtirol, for example, was renamed Alto Adige, a reference to the northern reaches of the Adige river. Nowadays it is a bilingual autonomous region, and place names appear in both languages everywhere from street signs to mountains.

In the adjoining regions – the Trentino to the south and the Veneto

in the south-east – Italian dominates. Just to complicate matters further, the ancient Ladin language, a hangover from pre-Roman times, is still the mother tongue of many inhabitants of the central Dolomite valleys of Badia, Gardena and Fassa, with additional pockets around Cortina and across Friuli.

Consequently, place-naming across the Dolomites is by no means standardised! For the purposes of this guide – and to avoid weighing the text down – place names are given in Italian, flanked by the German or Ladin version if they differ dramatically. One to watch out for is *Rifugio* (or *Hütte*), recently transformed into Ladin *Ücia* or *Ütia*.

GEOLOGY

The rocks of the Dolomites were formed some 230 million years ago, when a shallow tropical sea covered the area and remains of coral and sea creatures gradually built up on its floor, hardening over time into sedimentary rock. Much later, around 65 million years ago, land-moving tectonic events thrust the rock dramatically upwards, as the Alps were created. A succession of ice ages followed, and erosion from snow, rain and wind continues to shape the mountains.

However it took time for people to understand these events. The Monti Pallidi or 'Pale Mounts' as they were originally called, were rechristened

Fossilised Megalodonts in the 'cimitero dei fossili' (Walk 50)

in honour of a French mineralogist marquis with the unforgettable name Déodat Guy Sylvain Tancrède Gratet de Dolomieu. On a 1789 visit he identified the main rock as calcium magnesium carbonate (later known as 'dolomite' in his honour), and it shares the show with limestone, namely calcium carbonate.

Scholars continued to puzzle over the abundance of fossilised shells and marine creatures embedded in the rock at such heights and so far from the sea. In 1860, with the theory of the biblical Flood long rejected, Baron Ferdinand von Richthofen correctly proposed their genesis as a coral reef, work further developed by Edmund von Mojsisovics.

According to legend however, the dolomite rock is splendidly pale as it's coated with fine white gossamer woven from moon rays; at sundown it assumes gorgeous hues of orangey-pink, a delightful phenomenon known by the Ladin term *enrosadira*.

For more geology, plan a visit to the museums in Verona (https://museodistorianaturale.comune.verona.it), Cortina d'Ampezzo (https://musei.regole.it/Zardini/index.php) or Predazzo (https://www.muse.it/it/Pagine/default.aspx).

PLANTS AND FLOWERS

The Dolomites boast over 1400 species of glorious flowering plants. This

*Clockwise from top left: edelweiss;
exotic martagon lily; rare devil's claw;
trumpet gentians; brilliant orange
lily; Rhaetian poppies on scree*

is a fifth of the total found in Italy and these are reason enough to go walking. Throughout the summer months it's impossible not to be impressed by the colourful spreads, often in the most unlikely and unhospitable spots. Heading the list is the mythical edelweiss. Found in alpine meadows, its felt-like petals form delicate overlapping stars. While not especially eye-catching, its blanched aspect inspired the legend that it was brought down from the moon by a princess, to remind her of the pale lunar landscape for which she was pining away.

One of the earliest blooms to appear is the Alpine snowbell; its fragile fringed blue-lilac bells even sprout in snow patches thanks to an 'anti-freeze' carbohydrate. Never far away are hairy pasque flowers in white or yellow. Shady clearings are the best places to look for the rare, showy lady's slipper orchid, recognisable by its maroon petals around a swollen, yellow-lipped receptacle. Masses of purple orchids are common in meadows as are cone-shaped black vanilla orchids that smell like cocoa-vanilla close-up – according to alpine hearsay, cows that munch on them produce chocolate-flavoured milk! Fluttery scented Rhaetian poppies punctuate dazzling white scree slopes with their patches of bright

yellow-orange, never far from clumps of pink thrift or round-leaved pennycress, which is honey-scented. Another precious bloom is the less commonly encountered king-of-the-Alps, a striking cushion of bright blue blooms reminiscent of a dwarf version of forget-me-not. A rare treat is devil's claw which sports a segmented pointy lilac flower with curly pointed stigma that specialises in hanging off vertical rock faces. Another rock coloniser is saxifrage, the name literally 'rock breaker', so called for its deep-reaching roots. Pretty pink cinquefoil also blooms on stone surfaces, its delicate flowers scattered amid starry clusters of silvery-grey leaves.

Unmissable, fat and intensely deep blue trumpet gentians burst through the grass, demanding admiration, and there are also daintier star-shaped varieties. In lush meadows gorgeous orange and wine-red martagon lilies vie with each other for brilliance. Light larch woodland and stony grassed slopes are often colonised by alpenrose, rather like azaleas, with masses of pretty red-pink flowers in late July. Its neighbours are low bilberry bushes, laden with tiny sweet fruit in late summer.

A couple of flowering species are endemic to the Dolomites. Moretti's bellflower, with its rounded deep blue petals, nestles in rock crevices between 1500m and 2300m, while the succulent Dolomitic houseleek prefers sunny dry slopes and sports a bright green stalk and deep pink pointy flowers. It is just one of the houseleeks which bear an uncanny resemblance to miniature triffids.

A valuable aid to identification is the Cicerone pocket guide *Alpine Flowers* (2019).

In terms of trees, beech grow up to about the 1000m line before conifers take over. Silver fir and spruce mingle with Arolla pine, which can reach 2600m in altitude and is recognisable for its tufted needles, reddish bark and contorted trunk. Also of note is the springy low-lying dwarf mountain pine, a great coloniser of scree whose springy branches invade paths. A high achiever is larch, which grows up to 2500m. The sole non-evergreen conifer, with the onset of winter it loses its needles in a copper-tinged rain. On the other hand a remarkable 'bonsai' tree is net-leaved willow, whose closely packed root system creeps over rock surfaces.

WILDLIFE

One of the beauties of walking is the chance it gives you to observe the wild creatures that call these mountains home. As if the harsh environment and climate weren't enough, it's nothing short of a miracle that they survive and thrive despite man's efforts to dislodge them with roads, ski runs and resorts, not to mention large-scale sports events. Selective hunting is also allowed in some valleys, albeit under strict controls. The good news is that much of the Dolomites comes under the protection of nature parks – see below.

The easiest animals to see are playful alpine marmots: adorable furry social creatures a bit like beavers (without the flat tail), which forage for their favourite flowers and live in extensive underground colonies. Wary of foxes and golden eagles who can carry off the young, they always have a sentry posted, an older animal who stands rod-straight and emits heart-stopping warning whistles to summon the tribe back home. Marmots hibernate from October to April, waking once a month to urinate. They were once hunted throughout the Alps for their skins and fat, and paraded in street fairs.

Conifer woods provide shelter for roe and red deer, although often you only catch a fleeting glimpse of them due to their shyness. Higher up, rocky mountainsides and seemingly impossible cliff faces and scree slopes are the ideal terrain for shy herds of fleet-hoofed chamois, mountain goats with short crochet-hook horns and pale fawn coats. They often give themselves away by dislodging loose stones.

An impressive creature is the majestic ibex, sporting sturdy grooved horns that curve backwards up to a metre on males, who can weigh 100kg; the females less on both counts. Unlike deer, ibex (and chamois) don't lose their horns every year. Over-zealous hunters wiped them out back in the 1700s however they

Alpine marmot

were successfully re-introduced in the 1970s from a surviving group in the Valle d'Aosta, and a 2022 census counted 700 ibex in well-established herds. During the summer young males spend time in mock battle clashing their horns in preparation for the December mating season when it is anything but pretend, as the females are only on heat for 24 hours.

Mouflon are vaguely similar, though with curly horns. Small herds live in southern and western valleys. Hard to see, they feed at night and take rest in woodland by day.

Brown bears once roamed freely until they were hunted to near-extinction in the 1800s. Now protected, a dwindling group in the western Dolomites has been slowly boosted by bears from Slovenia – the latest head count is around 100. Sightings and fleeting encounters are becoming more common in the Trentino region, where they are an increasing nuisance for shepherds and beekeepers.

European wolves on the other hand have required no help at all. Originating from the central Italian Apennines, these elegant creatures have slowly but surely come north and spread across the Italian Alps. There are now reports of 20 packs across the Dolomites; when wild prey is unavailable, they do occasionally attack livestock.

In the extremely unlikely circumstance you see either a brown bear or a wolf, use your common sense and keep your distance. Do not approach, for any reason.

Birdwatchers will enjoy the delightful songbirds in woodland, while birds of prey such as kites and

Alpine chough

buzzards may be spotted above the tree line. One special treat is the *lammergeier* or bearded vulture, back in the Alps after centuries of persecution. Easy to recognise for its orange neck ruff and impressive three-metre wingspan, the bird glides low in search of an abandoned carcass: it extracts bones to drop on rocks, breaking them open to eat. In contrast the magnificent golden eagle, only marginally smaller, preys on small animals which it carries off in its sharp talons.

The gregarious Alpine chough, with its bright yellow beak, and the similar red-billed chough are types of crow that perform acrobatics in large flocks. Cheeky scavengers, they are aroused by the slightest rustle of a food wrapper, and appear out of nowhere to hover optimistically, sure

in the knowledge that all walkers stop at cols for a snack, leaving crumbs and apple cores behind (and hopefully nothing else).

Another feathered treat is the showy high-altitude wallcreeper. Fluttering like a butterfly over sheer rock faces in its hunt for spiders, it flashes its plumage (black with red panels and white dots) and attracts attention with its shrill piping call. There is also the ptarmigan, a type of high-mountain grouse that nests on grassy slopes and sounds a bit like a pig snorting. In winter, with a perfect white plumage camouflage, it can patter over snow surfaces without sinking thanks to fine hairs on its claws, akin to snowshoes. However, an undisputed bird queen is the cumbersome capercaillie, a dark-coloured ground dweller as big as a turkey. A rare sight for the lucky few in the conifer woods with their click-click courting call, a good bet to see one is in autumn when they scout for laden bilberry shrubs. An excellent guide-book is Bertel Bruun's *Hamlyn Guide to Birds of Britain and Europe*.

Even though terrible dragons have long been banished from the Alps by valorous knights, there are two potential dangers in terms of wildlife. The first is bites from ticks (*zecche* in Italian), which may carry Lyme's disease (*borreliosis*) and even TBE (tick-borne encephalitis), which can be life-threatening to humans. Warnings apply to the southern Dolomites in heavily wooded areas up to around 1500m altitude with thick under-growth where ticks can latch onto you. Sensible precautions include wearing long trousers and spraying boots, clothing and hat (but not skin!) with an insect repellent containing permethrin, and avoiding sitting in long grass. Inspect yourself carefully after a walk for suspect black spots or itching. Remove any ticks very care-fully using tweezers – be sure to get the head out – or a specialist tick-removal tool and disinfect the skin. Consult a doctor if you are concerned or experience any symptoms. For more information see www.lymene-teurope.org and https://ecdc.europa.eu/en/tick-borne-encephalitis.

The second warning concerns vipers (or adders): smallish, light grey-tawny snakes with a diamond-shaped head and zigzag patterned back. Their bite can be fatal, particularly for children and the elderly, but it is extremely rare. Although widespread, especially in abandoned pasture and old huts, they are timid creatures that slither away very quickly if they consider themselves to be in danger. They only attack if threatened, so if you meet one – on a path for exam-ple, where it is probably sunning itself and may be lethargic – give it ample time and room to move away. In the unlikely circumstance that some-one is bitten, stay put and seek help immediately.

NATURE PARKS

The first protected nature parks in the Dolomites date back to 1967: the Trentino province's marvellous Parco Naturale Paneveggio-Pale di San Martino www.parcopan.org and the vast Adamello-Brenta www.pnab.it. These were followed by a host of *parchi naturali* established as of 1974 across the northern swathe of the Dolomites under the Alto Adige (see https://nature-parks.provinz.bz.it). The first was the magnificent Sciliar-Catinaccio, then the beautiful Puez-Odle, wonderful Fanes-Senes-Braies and lastly the Tre Cime which encom-passes the majestic Sesto Dolomites. A little later, as local administra-tions became more environmentally enlightened, the Parco delle Dolomiti d'Ampezzo (www.dolomitiparco.com) came into being in the Cortina district in 1990. Then, in 1993, the vast Parco Nazionale Dolomiti Bellunesi (www.dolomitipark.it) was established, spreading across rugged ranges in the south. All have excellent visitor facilities, education programmes, forest and wildlife management and path upkeep.

GETTING THERE

The Dolomite mountains are in the far northeast of Italy, close to the border with Austria. Access from all directions is straightforward.

By plane

The nearest international airports in Italy are at Verona www.aeroporto verona.it, Treviso www.trevisoairport. it and Venice www.veniceairport.it. Otherwise in Austria there's Innsbruck www.innsbruck-airport.com. All have good ongoing bus or rail connections.

By train

International trains from Innsbruck and Munich via the Brenner Pass run to Bolzano, then continue to Trento and Verona. Alternately from the east, via Lienz in Austria, a minor line runs into Italy along Val Pusteria to Fortezza, just south of the Brenner.

Other lines from the south and Venice connect with Feltre, Belluno and Longarone, as well as Calalzo. See www.trenitalia.com and www. oebb.at for timetables and online booking. Rail passes make train travel an attractive option.

By bus

A host of long-distance coaches from major Italian cities provide direct links with the Dolomites throughout summer. All require booking – possible on websites and apps. See Appendix A.

By car

If you approach Italy from the north, the best entry point is by the Brenner Pass from Austria on the A22 *autostrada* (motorway). This leads directly to the northwestern Dolomites, with handy exits between Bressanone and Trento. Otherwise if you arrive from the west on the A4, exit before Verona and join the A22 heading northwards. From Venice, the A27 runs north via Vittorio Veneto to Longarone, with good roads continuing for Belluno and Cortina for the eastern Dolomites.

LOCAL TRANSPORT

The extensive network of trains and buses across the Dolomites is unfailingly reliable, easy to use and remarkably inexpensive. Visitors are warmly encouraged to make their Dolomites holiday car-free, without adding to air pollution and traffic congestion in these magical mountains. The 50 walks in this guidebook are accessible by public transport and the whole book was researched in this way. Strategically placed cable cars, gondola and chairlifts as well as shuttle minibuses and jeep taxis are also used.

The Rasciesa funicular (Walk 31)

Many lines operate year-round and generally speaking, summer timetables correspond to the Italian school holidays, which usually fall from mid-June to mid-September. Exact dates vary year to year, company to company and region to region. The main companies are Dolomiti Bus, SAD, Trentino Trasporti, Cortina Express as listed in the individual walk information box. See Appendix A for contact details and where to find timetables. Most let you buy your ticket on board though, where possible, it's best to purchase beforehand through the company app or ticket office to save delaying the bus or paying a surcharge (in the case of Dolomiti Bus).

The Italian rail company is Trenitalia. **Note:** Unless you have a booked seat (in which case your ticket will show a date and time) stamp your ticket in one of the machines on the platform before boarding. Failure to do so can result in a fine.

INFORMATION

Tourist offices are dotted all over the Dolomites and can help with transport info, accommodation and much more. See Appendix A for listings.

WHEN TO GO

The Dolomites! It was full fifteen years since I had first seen sketches of them by a great artist not long since passed away, and their strange outlines and still stranger colouring had haunted me ever since. I thought of them as every summer came round; I regretted them every autumn; I cherished dim hopes about them every spring.

Amelia Edwards (1873)

Don't put off your trip! Plan on visiting the Dolomites between May/June and October for walking, unless you're equipped for snow and ice. From early summer low-mid altitude walks are feasible, but for high altitude routes it's worth waiting until July so they're free of late-lying snow, as accumulations in gullies can conceal waymarking or harden into tricky ice. The *rifugi* or *Hütte* (mountain huts) open from late June through to late September/October, should you rely on them for meals or overnight accommodation, while summer bus lines, cable cars and lifts run from around mid June to September. August is the busiest month, focusing on 15 August, a key Italian holiday.

July tends to be the best month for flowers, while September to October have cooler conditions and superb visibility as autumn and its crispness approaches, with the odd chance of snowfall. This is a magical time for russet hues and golden 'rain' from the larch trees. Late-season walkers will be rewarded with improved chances of observing wildlife in solitude. Italy stays on summer time until the end of October, when there is daylight until about 6pm.

ACCOMMODATION

All the Dolomite valleys and villages offer an excellent choice of hotel (*albergo*), guesthouse (*locanda*), bed & breakfast (*affittacamera*, *Garnì*) and farm stay (*agriturismo*) options for all pockets. Families with children will appreciate the freedom of a house (*casa*) or flat (*appartamento*); rentals are common, usually on a weekly basis. In addition, well-equipped and well-located camping grounds abound.

Generally speaking reservation is not usually necessary outside the August to early September peak season, but all the same, it is advisable to book in advance to avoid disappointment and wasting time. If you're passing through, look for *camera libera* or *Zimmer frei* (room free) signs. Online accommodation agencies such as booking.com cover the Dolomites in great detail.

Each walk described in this guide can be completed in a single day, so that walkers can return to their valley accommodation. However an overnight stay in an alpine refuge is a memorable experience and can be the highlight of a walking holiday. It's worth trying to factor one in during a trip. With the odd exception at road level, these marvellous establishments are set in spectacular high-altitude positions accessible only to walkers or climbers. Contact details for huts visited in this guide are listed in Appendix B.

The mountain huts are open throughout the summer months

Rifugio Palmieri, also known as Croda da Lago (Walk 21)

(June–September/October) and offer reasonably priced meals and hostel-like sleeping facilities that range from spartan dormitories with bunk beds ·to cosy guest rooms. Charges start at around €18 for a bed and €55 for half board, which means overnight stay, a three-course dinner and breakfast.

The majority belong to the Club Alpino Italiano (CAI) along with the Trento branch SAT and Südtirol AVS (members and affiliates enjoy discounted rates as per reciprocal agreements), but lots are run by local families and alpine guides; in any case everyone is welcome to eat and stay.

Pillows and blankets or duvets are always provided, so sleeping bags are not needed. A sleeping sheet (bag liner), however, is compulsory in the club-run huts, so carry your own. You'll also need a small towel, not that showers (hot or cold) are common due to water shortages. Bathrooms and toilets are shared – loo paper is always provided. A pair of flip-flops is a good idea as you can't wear your boots inside. Hut rules include no smoking, and 'lights out' with silence from 10pm to 6am, when the generator is switched off.

Refuge accommodation should be booked in advance for July and August, especially on weekends. Most staff speak English but don't assume this. On the phone, say: *Vorrei prenotare un posto letto/due posti letto* ('I'd like to book one/two beds'). Some huts accept credit cards – check when you book – but it's best to carry a supply of euros in cash, to be on the safe side. All towns and large villages have an ATM.

FOOD AND DRINK

While this may not be the gastronomical heart of Italy, foodies will definitely not be disappointed. The northern valleys pride themselves on delicious cereal breads, such as *Völser Schüttelbrot*, crunchy rounds of unleavened rye with cumin seeds, or a softer yeasty version. Both are a perfect taste match for thinly sliced *Speck*, smoked ham flavoured with juniper berries, coriander and garlic.

Restaurant and refuge menus feature a mouth-watering range of traditional local dishes. *Knödeln* or *canederli*, farm-style dumplings the size of tennis balls are made of bread blended with eggs and flavoured with smoked ham, spinach or liver and served either in consommé or drenched with butter and parmigiano cheese. The choice of pasta will undoubtedly include the reliable classic *pasta con ragù*, with a rich sauce of minced meat and tomato. There may be gnocchi, tiny potato dumplings, or the Trentino version *strangolapreti* (priest stranglers!) made with spinach. If you're

Homemade ravioli

lucky the list will include *casunziei*, soft home-made ravioli pockets filled with beetroot and sprinkled with poppy seeds, or *Schlutzkrapfen*, stuffed with greens and ricotta cheese.

For a main course in the southern valleys, *tosella* – a fresh cheese (vaguely resembling mozzarella) lightly fried in butter or oven-baked with cream – is definitely worth tasting. There may also be *pastin*, a spicy sausage. Otherwise, go for *polenta con formaggio fuso*, corn meal smothered with melted cheese, hopefully accompanied by *funghi*, wild mushrooms. Meat eaters will enjoy the specialty *carne salada con fagioli*, thinly sliced cured beef with brown beans, if not the spicy goulash or *Bauernschmaus* which corresponds to smoked pork and sausages on a bed of warm *Sauerkraut*, stewed cabbage. Definitely not for mild

palates is pungent *Graukäse*, lumpy greyish farm cheese served with oil, vinegar and raw onion – be warned.

For walkers with a sweet tooth, the dessert front is dominated by *Kaiserschmarm*, a scrumptious concoction of sliced pancake with dried fruit and redcurrant jelly. Another special treat (and a meal in itself) is *Strauben*, fried squirts of sweetened batter with bilberry sauce. Ask at the bakeries for *Apfelstrudel* or *Mohnstrudel*, a luscious pastry roll stuffed with apple or poppy seeds respectively. October visitors will enjoy the freshly picked crunchy apples on sale in the Südtirol orchards.

Some memorable wines hail from the outskirts of the Dolomites. Among the reds are the full-bodied Teroldego and lighter Schiava from the Trentino, as well as excellent Lagrein and Blauburgunder (Pinot nero) from the slopes above Bolzano. The list

WATER

Water is relatively scarce throughout the Dolomites due to the porous dolomite and limestone rock – which implies that most surface water disappears underground – as well as the dearth of glaciers and permanent snowfields. The bottom line is – use it sparingly in the mountains and don't take it for granted. A general rule is to top up your bottle whenever possible. Water may occasionally not be drinkable – *acqua non potabile/kein Trinkwasser*. By all means carry a sterilising filter – all shapes and sizes are available on the market. Mineral water is always on sale in refuges though this inevitably involves polluting transport.

In towns and villages tap water (*acqua da rubinetto/Leitungswasser*) is guaranteed safe for drinking and is tested frequently; you can request it in restaurants and cafés.

of whites is headed by the heavenly, aromatic Gewürztraminer, which originated at Termeno (near Bolzano), while very drinkable Riesling and others are produced from grapes grown on the steep terraces over the Isarco valley.

The non-alcoholic *Holundersaft*, elderberry blossom drink, can be especially refreshing on a hot summer's day. Beer (*birra*) comes in all sorts of flavours, shades and sizes.

Coffee is strictly Italian-style and comes as short black espresso, milky frothy cappuccino or less concentrated *caffe latte*, as well as an infinite range of intermediate combinations. Tea is usually served black with lemon unless you specify *con latte* (with milk). A warming drink on a cold day is thick, rich *cioccolata calda* (hot chocolate).

WHAT TO TAKE

Essentials start with good quality waterproof boots with ankle support and non-slip soles – preferably not brand new, unless you plan on using lots of plasters! While normal trainers are totally inadequate for alpine paths, trail running shoes are a good lightweight option if you're used to them.

Second on the list is a comfortable rucksack, big enough to contain food and drink for a day, along with extra clothing, rain gear and emergency items including a first aid kit. Shoulder bags are totally unsuitable and can be dangerous.

A wide-brimmed hat, sunglasses and high-factor protective sun cream are essential – remember that for every 1000m of ascent, the intensity of the sun's UV rays increases by 10 per cent.

Layers of clothing are needed to cater for fiery sun through to wind, lashing rain, storms and even snow.

Lightweight telescopic trekking poles come in handy on steep slopes, especially for wonky knees.

Although food is available at huts on the majority of walks described in this guidebook, it is best to be self-sufficient. Bad weather, minor accidents and all manner of unforeseen factors could hold you up on the track, and that extra biscuit or energy bar could become crucial.

Mineral salt tablets are helpful in combating salt depletion and dehydration caused by profuse sweating; unexplained prolonged fatigue and symptoms similar to heat stroke indicate a problem.

MAPS

An excellent network of paths covers the Dolomites, each marked with frequently placed red and white paint stripes on prominent fence posts, tree trunks and rocks, and complete with a distinguishing number, shown on commercial walking maps. While 1:50,000 scale maps are provided in this guide, limitations of space make it impossible to include full details, which are essential in an emergency,

The Gores de Federa route signed at Col Purin (Walk 20)

or Stanfords (www.stanfords.co.uk) in the UK if you prefer to purchase them beforehand.

Note: Walkers will inevitably find discrepancies between the names used in this book and those on sign-posts and maps as cartographers and local authorities reintroduce dialect names and remove longer estab-lished versions – not always a helpful practice.

See Appendix C for an Italian–German–English glossary of terms.

DOS AND DON'TS

It's better to arrive early and dry, than late and wet
Age-old alpine wisdom

so it is recommended that walkers obtain the relative maps listed in indi-vidual walk information boxes. These are the Tabacco 1:25,000 series; the app for digital maps is downloadable from www.tabaccomapp.it.

However a more economical, if slightly less detailed option, is the excellent Kompass 1:35,000 series; the n.672 pack of four maps covers the whole of the Dolomites with the exception of the Brenta Dolomites in the west (covered by the 1:25000 n.073 map). All available from www.kompass-italia.it.

The maps are sold throughout the Dolomites and leading overseas booksellers include Omnimap in the US (www.omnimap.com), and the Map Shop (www.themapshop.co.uk)

- Find time to get in shape before setting out on your holiday, as a good level of fitness will maximise enjoyment. If you're exhausted, you probably won't appreciate the wonderful scenery and won't react well in an emergency
- On the trail, find your pace. If you have to keep stopping to catch your breath, you're going too fast
- Don't be overly ambitious; choose routes suited to your capacity and read the walk description before setting out. If you suffer from ver-tigo, avoid walks with exposure. Never hesitate to turn back if the route doesn't look like your cup of tea
- Get into the habit of leav-ing word at your hotel of your

planned route, or signing the hut register if staying in a refuge, as this may be helpful in search and rescue if you don't turn up when expected

- Start out early in the morning to give yourself plenty of daylight. Never set out late and always keep extra time up your sleeve to allow for possible detours due to collapsed bridges, wrong turns and missing signposts. In hot weather plan on getting to your destination early as afternoon storms are not uncommon
- Stick with your companions and don't lose sight of them. Remember that the progress of groups matches that of the slowest member
- Avoid walking in brand new footwear as it may cause blisters, but leave those worn-out boots in the shed, as they may prove unsafe on slippery terrain. Three-quarters of mountain accidents are caused by slipping so choose your footwear carefully!
- Don't overload your rucksack and remember that drinking water and food add extra weight
- Carry extra protective clothing as well as energy foods for emergency situations. Remember that in normal circumstances the temperature drops an average of 6°C for every 1000m you climb
- Check the weather forecast if possible – tourist offices and hut guardians are in the know. For

the Südtirol see https://weather. provinz.bz.it, for Trentino www. meteotrentino.it and for the Veneto www.arpa.veneto.it. Never set out on a long route in adverse conditions. Even a broad track can become treacherous in bad weather, and high-altitude terrain enveloped in thick mist makes orientation difficult

- Learn the international distress signal (see Mountain safety box). DO NOT rely on your mobile phone, as there may not be any signal. All refuges have a reliable phone and experienced staff can always be relied on in an emergency
- During an electrical storm, don't shelter under trees or rock overhangs, and keep away from metallic fixtures
- Please carry rubbish back to the valley, where it can be disposed of correctly; don't expect hut or park staff to deal with it. Even organic waste such as apple cores and orange peel is best not left lying around, as it upsets the diets of animals and birds
- Be considerate when making a toilet stop. Abandoned huts and rock overhangs could serve as life-saving shelter for someone. If you must use paper or tissues, carry it away; the small lightweight bags used by dog owners are perfect. There is no excuse for leaving unsightly toilet paper anywhere

ALPINE CLUBS

Membership of CAI (Club Alpino Italiano) is open to Italians and people of all nationalities. Prospective members need to apply to individual branches; the complete list can be found at www.cai.it. The annual fee is around €50, with half-price rates for family members and less for children. As well as reductions at huts throughout the Alps, membership includes alpine rescue insurance. Otherwise Brits can join the UK branch of the Austrian club (www.aacuk.org.uk), and for North Americans there's the Alpine Club of Canada (www.alpineclubofcanada.ca) and the US equivalent (https://americanalpineclub.org).

- Collecting flowers, insects or minerals is strictly forbidden, as is lighting fires
- Get a handy app like PeakFinder which helps put names to all those weird and wonderful mountains, which will quickly become good companions
- Lastly, use common sense in all situations

EMERGENCIES

For medical matters, walkers who live in the EU need a European Health Insurance Card (EHIC) while UK residents require a UK Global Health Insurance Card (GHIC) once their EHIC card has expired. Holders of both are entitled to free or subsidised emergency treatment in Italy, which has an excellent public health system. Australia has a reciprocal agreement – see www.medicareaustralia.gov.au. Those from other countries should make sure they have appropriate cover.

Travel insurance to cover an alpine walking holiday is also strongly recommended, as costs in the case of rescue and repatriation can be hefty.

'Help!' in Italian is 'Aiuto!' (pronounced 'eye-yoo-toh') in Italian, and 'Hilfe!' (pronounced 'hilfer') in German.

Italy's general emergency telephone number is 112, while calls for soccorso alpino (mountain rescue) need to be made to 118.

The international rescue signals can come in handy: the call for help is six signals per minute. These can be visual (such as waving a handkerchief or flashing a torch) or audible (whistling or shouting). Repeat after a one-minute pause. The answer is three visual or audible signals per minute, to be repeated after a one-minute pause. Anyone who sees or hears a call for help must contact the nearest refuge or police station as quickly as possible.

USING THIS GUIDE

Each walk description is preceded by an information box containing the following essential data (values for any route extensions or alternatives are stated in brackets):

- **Distance** in kilometres.
- **Ascent and Descent** This is important information, as height gain and loss are a further indication of the effort required and these figures need to be taken into account alongside difficulty grade and distance when planning the day. A walker of average fitness will usually cover 300m in ascent in one hour.
- **Difficulty** The difficulty of each walk is classified by grade, although adverse weather conditions will make any route more arduous. Even a level road can be treacherous if icy.
  - Grade 1 – an easy route on clear tracks and paths, suitable for beginners
  - Grade 2 – paths across typical mountain terrain, often rocky and with considerable ups and downs, where a reasonable level of fitness is preferable
  - Grade 3 – strenuous, often entailing exposed stretches and extra climbs. Experience and extra care are recommended
- **Walking time** This does not include pauses for picnics, views, photos or nature stops, so always add on a good couple of hours when planning your day. Times given during the descriptions are partial (as opposed to cumulative). If following a route in the opposite direction, allow roughly

two-thirds of the time if it's an ascent that you're descending, and about 1½ times more for a downhill section that you're climbing up.

- **Note** A handful of walks described have moderately exposed stretches across rock faces aided by anchored cable. Known as *sentiero attrezzato* (as opposed to a via ferrata aided climbing route where experience, helmet and harness are compulsory), they do not strictly necessitate special equipment, but there are rules to be followed:
  - Always keep away from iron cables and rungs in bad weather and if a storm is brewing, as the fixtures attract lightning
  - Avoid two-way traffic on a single stretch of cable, as it can become awkward and consequently dangerous if you try to pass people. It's common sense to wait until those approaching from the opposite direction have passed before you proceed, to avoid any added strain on cables

In the walk descriptions compass bearings are in abbreviated form (N, S, NNW and so on) as are directions right (R) and left (L). Reference landmarks and key places encountered en route are in bold type, with their altitude in metres above sea level given as 'm', not to be confused with minutes (abbreviated as 'min').

THE WALKS

The Campanile di Popena bears a curious resemblance to the hat traditionally worn by the Venetian rulers, the doges (Walk 12)

WALK 1
Lago di Braies

Start/Finish	Hotel Lago di Braies
Distance	3.5km
Ascent/Descent	50m
Grade	1
Walking time	1hr 30min
Map	Tabacco n.031 scale 1:25,000
Refreshments	Café-restaurants at Lago di Braies
Access	Lago di Braies can be reached on the SAD bus from Dobbiaco via Villabassa – booking may be compulsory between July and early September at www.prags.bz. If you drive in, expect hefty fees at the lake's car parks.
Note	The road is closed once the car parks are full.

This delightful *Giro del Lago* (lake circuit) consists of an easy anti-clockwise stroll, alternating waterside stretches with woodland brightened by alpenrose shrubs. For a longer, more demanding route, see Walk 2.

LAGO DI BRAIES

Romantic Lago di Braies (aka Pragser Wildsee) is a top contender for 'most beautiful lake in the Dolomites' – not to mention most popular. Located in the Fanes-Sennes-Braies Nature Park it boasts deep emerald-green waters bound by bleached shingle beaches and sheer cliffs. The 31-hectare lake is fed by both alpine streams and underground springs. Trout survive in the chilly depths which plunge to 36m, while the surface temperature rarely exceeds 14 degrees Celsius – not inviting for a dip. As a rule it ices over in late November, not reverting to liquid form until May.

Popular for old-style boating, it was the set for the aptly named Italian soap opera *Un passo dal cielo* (One Step from Heaven). Lying at the foot of towering 2810m Croda del Beco, which is reflected on the still surface, it owes its existence to rockfalls that barred the valley. The name Braies may derive from the Celtic *bracu* (a marsh or swamp) if not from the Ladin *brage* (trousers), as the eponymous valley forks evenly into trouser legs.

A marvellous, rambling establishment occupies the northernmost end of the lake – the grand grey stone hotel built in 1899. In the 1960s it hosted meditation sessions with Maharishi Mahesh Yogi, the Beatles' personal guru. It is still a marvellous place as old-style furnishings have been retained and meals are taken in the spacious Art Nouveau dining rooms.

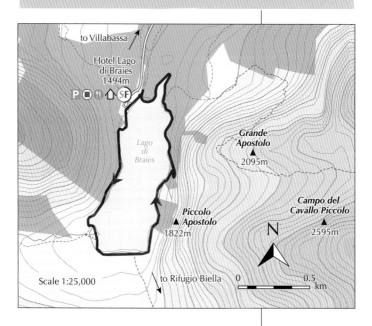

From the bus stop and car park, go R past Hotel Lago di Braies (1494m) to where a clutch of signposts point you L on n.1/4. The wide, level gravel path strikes out S past a chapel to follow the western edge of the lake, shaded by towering pine trees. Ignore the fork R for n.19 to Grünwald Alm and veer L for the path along a beach backed with dwarf mountain pines. You enjoy a stunning view of Croda del Beco.

LEGEND OF CRODA DEL BECO

According to an old Ladin legend, every 100 years on a full moon night, Princess Dolasilla and her blind mother the Queen of Fanes leave their dwelling beneath the Sass dla Porta (aka Croda del Beco) via a secret doorway. They row across the Braies lake in the hope of hearing silver trumpets announce the rebirth of their kingdom. Alas, they row in vain.

After a delightful amble, the route bears E along the top end of the lake. You pass the branch climbing to Rifugio Biella, and keep to the water's edge below remarkable rivers of scree. Directly opposite the hotel now, this is a marvellous spot for a dip on a sultry summer's day, though only for the courageous!

Boating on Lago di Braies

Rounding the lake's corner for the northward leg, you soon find yourself in light deciduous wood beneath the rocky mass of the Piccolo Apostolo. After a modest waterfall, a series of steps and raised timber walkways lead round a picturesque rocky point below the Grande Apostolo, with a lovely view over the lake.

Soon, the path loops around a slender outreached finger of shallow backwater edged by yellow marsh marigolds. You then pass the photogenic landing stage with rowing boats before returning to **Hotel Lago di Braies**. ▸

As a suitable follow-up, embark on an exploratory scull over the water or treat yourself to tea or an aperitif in the hotel garden.

WALK 2
Rifugio Biella Loop

Start/Finish	Hotel Lago di Braies
Distance	16km
Ascent/Descent	950m
Grade	2
Walking time	5hr 50min
Map	Tabacco n.031 scale 1:25,000
Refreshments	Lago di Braies, Rifugio Biella
Access	Lago di Braies can be reached on the SAD shuttle bus from Dobbiaco via Villabassa – booking may be compulsory between July and early September at www. prags.bz. If driving, expect hefty fees at lake car parks.
Note	The road is closed once the car parks are full.

If an excursion is made to Ausser Brags, a noble view is presented of the massive square-edged wall of the See Kofel, impending over a small lake, and rising to a height of 9,200 feet.... Its dark form, as seen from Cortina, when backed by storm clouds, looks marvellously like a gigantic elephant uprearing itself.

J Gilbert and GC Churchill (1864)

The 'elephant' Croda del Beco in Italian – Seekofel in German and Sass dla Porta in Ladin – dominates this walk, which starts out from the 'small lake' Lago di Braies. It is postcard pretty with turquoise-emerald waters alive with trout and fringed with beaches and imposing cliffs. See Walk 1 for more.

The walk itself is an exciting circuit, but it is lengthy and tiring. Set out early, don't underestimate the climb and carry plenty of drinking water and sun protection. You follow the opening stage of popular long-distance Alta Via 1 (AV1) as far as Rifugio Biella, a great spot for lunch. Then comes a quiet loop across rocky terrain where rock grouse nest among myriad wildflowers such as pink cinquefoil which miraculously take root in precious handfuls of wind-carried soil.

From the bus stop and car park, go R past Hotel Lago di Braies (1494m) to where a clutch of signposts point you L on n.1 (for Rifugio Biella). The broad gravel path heads S past a chapel to follow the western edge of the lake, shaded by pines. Ignore the fork R for n.19 to Grünwald Alm and veer L for the path along a beach that gives awesome views of massive Croda del Beco.

After a delightful amble, the route bears E at the top end of the lake to the key fork (**30min**) where n.1/AV1 breaks off R in ascent crossing extensive scree flows where flowers and dwarf mountain pines have taken root. You climb steadily, zigzags taking the sting out of the slope to where a wooden walkway and cable help to round a crumbling cliff face. It's not far up to a **junction** (2034m) with path n.4, the return route. Keep straight ahead on n.1 for the time being.

The wood is thicker and shadier now, the lake left well behind. An amphitheatre leads to an imposing rock barrier which is surmounted on a relentless zigzag path aided by fixed chains. Take your time and watch your step. Ignore a fork L (2186m, path n.3) before the path enters the corridor aptly named **Forno**, which is a 'furnace' or heat trap on scorching summer days when the towering cliffs of Monte Muro block out any hopes of a breeze. After weaving your way through toppled rocks,

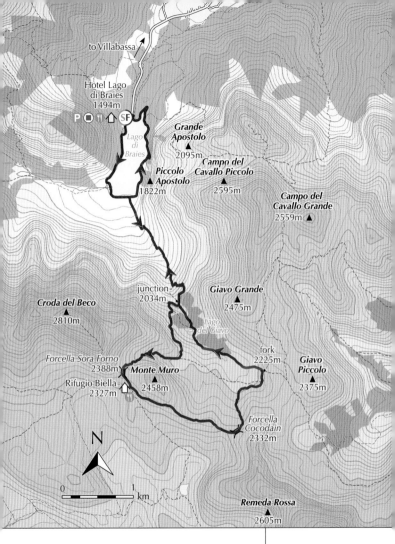

you eventually emerge at a pass with a shrine, **Forcella Sora Forno** (2388m), overlooking a vast plateau.

A 10min descent is all that separates you from the cream stone building **Rifugio Biella** (2327m, **2hr 50min**), an exemplary old-style refuge where generous slices of mouth-watering home-made tarts and Apfelstrudel are hard to resist. ◄

Walk 4 also comes here.

Now path n.28 leads SE in gentle ascent to an airy rocky crest studded with edelweiss and boasting wonderful views. As you're a little way back from Croda del Beco now, its regular onion-skin layers of limestone are clearer, as is the crazily tilted 45° angle. Watch your step as the way is pitted with hollows. Not far from the foot of imposing Remeda Rossa is **Forcella Cocodain** (2332m, **30min**). Here a faint route with occasional waymarking veers due N clambering over regular rock strata to join path n.3 and turn R. Only metres away, at a **fork** (2225m) it's L (NW) on n.4 into a pasture basin often populated by cows. The valley narrows after passing diminutive Lago del Giavo, then you drop to rejoin n.1 at the **junction** (**1hr**).

Go R and retrace your earlier steps in descent via the cable and walkway. Once back at the water's edge, keep R for the delightful path along the lake's rocky eastern shore. You pass a waterfall before a raised walkway leads round a rocky point, followed by a marshy stretch back to **Hotel Lago di Braies** (**1hr**).

Rifugio Biella backed by the Croda Rossa

WALK 3
Monte Specie

Start/Finish	Pratopiazza
Distance	8km (+8km for extension to Picco di Vallandro)
Ascent/Descent	340m (+848m for extension to Picco di Vallandro)
Grade	1–2 (2–3 for extension)
Walking time	2hr 45min (+4hr for extension to Picco di Vallandro)
Maps	Tabacco n.03 or n.010 scale 1:25,000
Refreshments	Pratopiazza, Malga Pratopiazza, Rifugio Vallandro
Access	Year-round SAD buses run from Dobbiaco to Ponticello. From here the final 7km to Pratopiazza is a narrow, limited-traffic toll road, served by shuttle bus most months. There are car parks at Ponticello and Pratopiazza.

Set almost 2000m above sea level and soaked in sunshine, Pratopiazza/ Plätzwiese is a perfect alpine basin dotted with photogenic timber chalets and red-barked Arolla pines and inhabited by contented dairy cows. Included in the Fanes-Sennes-Braies Nature Park it doubles as a splendid cross-country ski arena in winter, with the bonus appeal of being bounded by spectacular Dolomites, especially the Croda Rossa.

The walk visits wonderfully panoramic 2307m Monte Specie. Also known as Strudelkopf or Heimkehrerkreuz, this self-effacing promontory is a superb vantage point, especially over the Sesto Dolomites. Try and be there late afternoon to catch the shadows and colours.

A tougher walk (Grade 2–3, 4hr) entailing 848m in height gain heads for neighbouring Picco di Vallandro, aka Dürrenstein. The astonishingly panoramic sloping slab terminates with a dramatic pointed 2839m peak. The final stretch is exposed and requires a sure foot – see the extension below.

Alongside Rifugio Pratopiazza (1991m) clear well-trodden path n.40 forks E past a chapel on a gentle ascent through pasture with grazing cows. Ignore a fork L (for

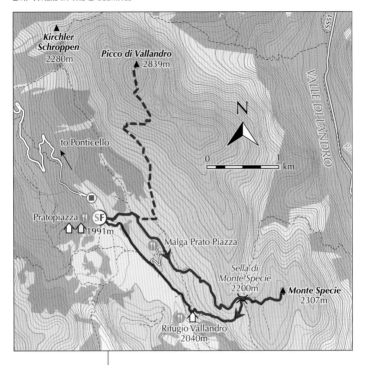

the Kirchler climbing area – *palestra di roccia*), but not far up branch R on n.40A. This leads SE across flowered slopes to bustling summer dairy farm-cum-café **Malga Prato Piazza** and its herds. Here you're pointed L again (still 40A) and over a fence into a side valley to an unusual timber covered bridge-cum-aqueduct. Keep uphill, enjoying a constantly improving outlook over the Pratopiazza basin and the magnificent Croda Rossa.

You join n.34, an old military road with a rough white stone surface and wind easily upwards SE. After a ridge, ruined WW1 barracks are located at the saddle **Sella di Monte Specie** (2200m). The final leg to the top – recognisable due E with its cross – cuts obliquely up a slope. At the very last moment the rounded top of

Monte Specie (2307m, **1hr 30min**) reveals its breathtaking magic: ahead is the wild Rondoi-Baranci group then the Tre Cime, slender and sharp like knife-blades from here. A handy orientation table puts names to all the mountains you can see.

Retrace your steps to the **Sella di Monte Specie** then leave the track by forking L on the *sentiero*. The straightforward path descends W over grassy terrain colonised by dwarf mountain pines before curving R via rock outcrops and dropping to friendly **Rifugio Vallandro** (2040m, **45min**). ▶

Turn R (NW) along the dirt road (n.37) for the scenic stroll flanking the pastoral basin to return to **Pratopiazza** (**30min**).

Arolla pines above Pratopiazza, looking over to the Croda Rossa

Close-by are the castle-like ruins of a prominent Austrian fort, witness to the activity here during the 1915–18 conflict.

53

Extension to Picco di Vallandro (4hr return)

From **Rifugio Pratopiazza** follow path n.40 uphill, ignoring turn-offs for n.40A, Malga Prato Piazza and Monte Specie. It's a very drawn-out but extremely rewarding ascent N up the vast sloping incline. The perfect path gradient and wide zigzags mean you hardly notice the climb, and can enjoy the ever-improving views to the Croda Rossa and Cristallo. Flowers and marmots add to the distractions.

A dizzy crest is finally gained at the 2700m mark. Even if you decide to make this the destination of your walk instead of carrying on to the peak, it's still well worth coming. The concluding stretch means a short but exposed neck with a fixed chain, terminating at the summit and cross of **Picco di Vallandro** (2839m, **2hr 30min**). A stunning spot looking over the Austrian Alps, Val Pusteria, the Sesto Dolomites and much more. Well done!

Retrace your steps to **Rifugio Pratopiazza** (**1hr 30min**).

WALK 4
Alpe di Sennes Circuit

Start/Finish	Rifugio Malga Ra Stua
Distance	17km (15km for short cut to Campo Croce)
Ascent/Descent	830m (600m for short cut to Campo Croce)
Grade	1–2
Walking time	5hr 15min (3hr for short cut to Campo Croce)
Map	Tabacco n.03 scale 1:25,000
Refreshments	Rifugio Malga Ra Stua, Rifugio Fodara Vedla, Rifugio Sennes, Rifugio Biella
Access	On the main road, Sant'Uberto and its car park mark the beginning of the narrow 3km road to Ra Stua. This is closed to traffic July–September, and the distance covered by a shuttle bus from the Dolomiti d'Ampezzo Park office at Fiames (local bus stop). Allow 40min on foot.

Embracing a marvellous range of scenery and habitats this is a lovely wander through neighbouring nature parks – Dolomiti d'Ampezzo and Fanes-Sennes-Braies. Grandiose mountains are stand-outs, their lower flanks cloaked by flourishing woods in a mix of deciduous species and evergreen conifer, including magnificent giant Arolla pines 400 years old!

The outward stages of the walk follow clear tracks and paths over undulating terrain, while the conclusion is a rather steep path – easily avoided by shortcutting back via Val Salata (see below). Families will enjoy this route if they ever get past Campo Croce where attractive gurgling streams act as a magnet on youngsters. Four particularly hospitable huts are touched on, marvellous lunch or refreshment stops.

A superb follow-up is a visit to the nearby Cascata di Fanes (access to a belvedere is signposted from Sant'Uberto). With its 70m drop, this is the highest waterfall in the Dolomites.

Rifugio Malga Ra Stua (1668m) is a comfortable hut-cum-dairy farm set in a picturesque pasture basin bounded by Croda Rossa and Lavinores.

STUA

Dotted with photogenic timber huts, this basin became a vast spread of Austrian tents during WW1. The name *stua* comes from 'dam', as the Torrente Boite was exploited to operate machinery for a medieval quarry of red stone. Local shepherds also diverted streams to curb the impetuous flow and access drinking water for their flocks.

Take the main track (n.6) N to **Campo Croce** (1758m, **20min**), where marshland is fed by meanders of the Torrente Boite. Here turn L on stony n.9, a wartime mule track.

The track winds its steady way W through Arolla pine and larch, levelling out to traverse lovely grassy basins dotted with dwarf mountain pines, the perfect habitat for both marmots and shy chamois. ▸ You pass a puddle-sized lake backed by the impressive Lavinores slabs, a tad before the delightful basin housing a batch of old timber huts and **Rifugio Fodara Vedla** (1966m, **1hr**), with a lovely view east to Croda Rossa.

Karstification is widespread, with grooved rock surfaces and sinkholes.

Giavo Grande 2475m

Croda del Beco 2810m

Rifugio Biella 2327m

▲ Monte Muro 2458m

Col de Lasta (Gran) ▲ 2311m

Rifugio Sennes 2126m

VAL SALATA

Lago di Fosses 2162m

Rem Ro 260

to San Vigilio di Marebbe

Rifugio Pédraces

Rifugio Fodara Vedla 1966m

Campo Croce 1758m

Torrente Boîte

Rifugio Malga Ra Stua 1668m

SF

Lavinores 2462m

N

0   1 km

to Sant'Ubert

Turn R on the jeep track n.7 uphill to where a path branches R through shrubs, climbing over a panoramic ridge. The jeep track is rejoined R before a path short cuts L via a crucifix for the last leg to hospitable **Rifugio Sennes** (2126m, **40min**). It is set in apparently bare surrounds although these are clearly satisfactory for the herds of robust cows.

At this point, should the final section look too long and tiring, by all means take the short cut to Campo Croce.

Val Salata short cut to Campo Croce (45min)
A short distance downhill E of **Rifugio Sennes** is the fork for the straightforward jeep track (n.6A) that drops easily SE down Val Salata under the line of cliffs that sweep down from the Remeda Rossa plateau. The source of the River Boite, which waters Cortina and later joins the Piave, is on the final stretch to **Campo Croce**.

Main route
Leave **Rifugio Sennes** uphill due N but soon turn R for path n.6 cutting over a ridge NE. You are accompanied by

The lovely Lago di Fosses basin backed by Croda del Beco

masses of gentians, edelweiss and marmots, and Croda del Beco can be admired with its trademark shiny grey inclined slabs. It's a gradual drop to join the lane heading L (E) to traditional-style **Rifugio Biella** (2327m, **1hr**), the panorama embracing the Tofane and Pelmo. This hut can also be visited on Walk 2.

The tarns here formed in layers of peat over a waterproof clay base.

From the hut's flagpole n.26 picks its way through the rocks SSE. Across open terrain where rock ptarmigan nest, you drop to lovely **Lago di Fosses** (2162m, **45min**) in the shade of layered Remeda Rossa. ◄

Once past the far end of the lake, signposts point you SE for a brief rise and saddle that accesses a desolate side valley at the foot of impressive Piccola Croda Rossa. A further lake, Lago di Remeda Rossa, is often dried up. Shortly, the clear path cuts down diagonally R (S) into a lovely flowered basin then dwarf mountain pines and a rough, tiring descent over loose rocks. You eventually emerge on the jeep track at **Campo Croce** (**1hr 15min**), which leads L to **Rifugio Malga Ra Stua** (**15min**).

Rifugio Fodara Vedla and the Croda Rossa

WALK 5

Landro to Cortina on the
Old Railway Line

Start/Finish	Gasthof Drei Zinnen/Cortina d'Ampezzo
Distance	20km
Ascent	120m
Descent	350m
Grade	1
Walking time	4hr 30min
Map	Tabacco n.03 scale 1:25,000
Refreshments	Gasthof Drei Zinnen, Lago di Landro, Carbonin, Cimabanche, Ospitale, Cortina
Access	The Gasthof is 1km N of Lago di Landro and can be reached by year-round SAD Cortina–Dobbiaco bus or the summer Cortina Express run.

This walk describes the 20km stretch from Landro to Cortina of the old railway line. A broad track is followed the whole way, with trifling height gain and loss. A string of bus stops (on short detours) enable you to bail out or slot in at will, and there's a handful of inviting café-restaurants. Long stretches of peaceful woodland home to deer and chamois complete the picture. (The 10km Dobbiaco–Landro leg is also feasible, however it tends to hug the road; much of the 30km section to Pieve di Cadore near Calalzo is worthwhile, even though it runs close to villages.)

Hard to believe, but the walk start was once a bustling village with a grand hotel. The quaint houses of Landro were adorned with timber façades and balconies, all demolished by Austrian forces. Nowadays there's the Gasthof Drei Zinnen, superbly set opposite a renowned viewpoint to the stunning Tre Cime di Lavaredo/Drei Zinnen, described from this angle as 'an apparition of three splintered spires' by the celebrated English writers and alpine travellers J Gilbert and GC Churchill (1864).

OLD RAILWAY LINE

In 1915 the Austrian army mapped out the narrow gauge Cortina–Dobbiaco railway line with imminent war in mind. After the conflict, work was completed in 1919 by the Italians, who extended it southeast from Cortina to Calalzo. Electrified in 1929, the line operated up until 1964 when bus transport took over. However the train – and Cortina railway station – can still be admired in the classic 1963 Peter Sellers film, *The Pink Panther*.

Although track and sleepers were later torn up, bridges and station buildings were left standing and the route is popular with cross-country skiers and mountain bikers. Walkers too can make the most of this marvellous leisurely piste with changing outlooks onto some impressive Dolomite groups.

From Gasthof Drei Zinnen (1406m) take the clear lane heading S, parallel to the road to **Lago di Landro** (bus stop, **15min**). Overshadowing the shallow body of green-white water is Monte Piana, fiercely contested during

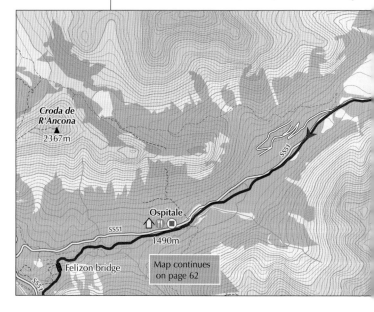

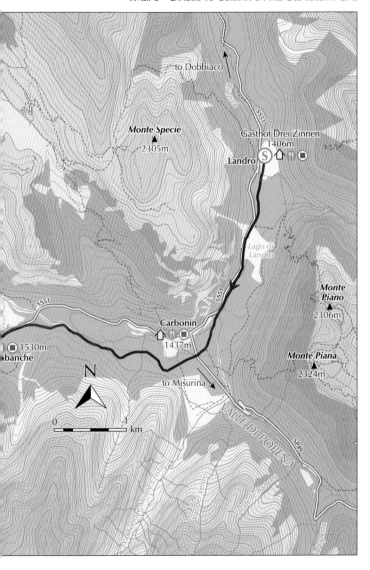

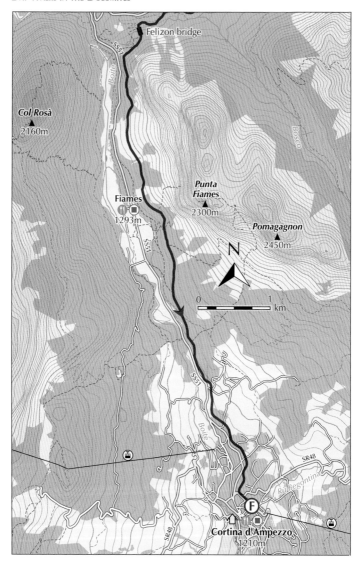

Felizon bridge

SS51

Boite

Col Rosà
2160m

Bosco

Punta Fiames
2300m

Fiames
1293m

SS51

Pomagagnon
2450m

N

0   1
km

SS51

Boite

SR48

RioBegontina

SR48

F

Cortina d'Ampezzo
1210m

WWI (see Walk 10). ▶ The track moves along the water's edge, marked by the truncated concrete blocks for pylons. After a gravel stream bed, it goes off into mixed wood, heading in the direction of the impressive Cristallo massif.

An underpass drops below the Misurina road (**30min**). Here a 5min detour R leads to **Carbonin** (1437m, bus stop, café-restaurant, hotel). Charcoal burners once worked in the vicinity, hence the name. ▶

As the track proceeds W, through the trees you can admire the Croda Rossa. Two bridges over rivers of scree precede key watershed **Cimabanche** (1530m, bus stop, **45min**), which marks the end of the gentle climb. Once the Austrian–Italian front, it now divides German-speaking Südtirol from the Italian-language Veneto region. However, of more immediate interest will be the tempting aroma of barbecued delights wafting from the outdoor café not far from the old station building.

From here on is gentle descent with fleeting glimpses of the Tofane. After a clutch of abandoned military buildings and a bus stop, the track passes a couple of lakes with

This northern sector was controlled by the Austrians and supplied from the lake by mechanised cableway, hence the wheel memorial here.

Starting out in 1836 as a modest inn for timber hauliers, the hotel here was transformed into a majestic summer retreat hosting VIPs, such as composer Gustav Mahler.

A fleeting glimpse of the marvellous Tofane is enjoyed after Ospitale

wild ducks. At the foot of awesome Vecio del Forame, it runs parallel to the road as far as **Ospitale** (1490m, bus stop, **1hr**). Here stand a 13th-century frescoed chapel and a former pilgrim hospice, now an atmospheric café-restaurant and guesthouse.

Below Croda de R'Ancona you move away from the traffic once again. Keep your eyes peeled for chamois on the opposite bank of the river – the steep scrubby rock terrain is their playground. After a short tunnel you cross the wartime **Felizon rail bridge**. Quite a piece of history with its criss-cross struts, it straddles jagged cliffs 70m above a chasm.

The track bears S and around a corner to enter a well-lit cavernous tunnel. A marvellous section. Once outside,

The route enters a short tunnel before the Felizon

you can see the milky blue of the Torrente Boite below. The track now traverses swathes of dwarf mountain pine interrupted by immense flows of scree at the foot of the towering Pomagagnon, with attractive shades of pink-red and grey-cream.

Further on a branch drops to nearby **Fiames** (1293m, bus stop, hotel/restaurant) but you continue on past an old station and through larch wood before the residential zone and **Cortina d'Ampezzo** itself (1210m, 2hr). You emerge directly at the bus terminal, easily recognisable as the former railway station.

WALK 6
Torre dei Scarperi Circuit

Start/Finish	Antoniusstein car park, Val Campo di Dentro
Distance	13.5km
Ascent/Descent	1019m
Grade	2
Walking time	5hr 30min
Maps	Tabacco n.010 scale 1:25,000
Refreshments	Rifugio Tre Scarperi
Access	By SAD bus from Sesto as far as Val Campo di Dentro (bus stop and car park), then on the summer shuttle to Antoniusstein, as the road is closed summer long. Otherwise allow 1hr on path n.105.

This exhilarating loop walk leads through the superb landscapes of the Sesto Dolomites, initially dominated by the massive Punta Tre Scarperi. It involves a hefty climb and return descent, along with an aided scramble (a short but not exposed stretch). The majority of the walk is straightforward but extremely enjoyable and highly panoramic as you skirt the central basin and admire the north face of the magnificent Tre Cime di Lavaredo formation. A single hut is encountered, close to the start, so set out equipped with food and drink.

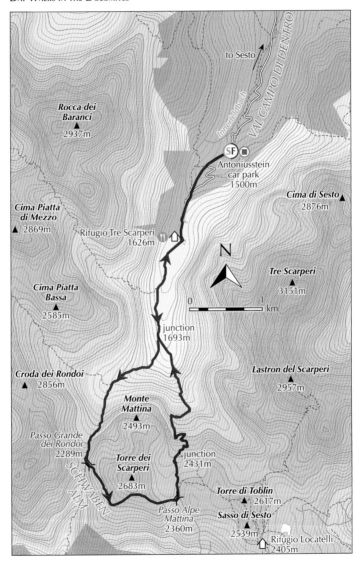

Awesome mountains and scree flows surround Campo di Dentro

From the Antoniusstein car park (1500m), a lovely path breaks off the road and climbs easily S to **Rifugio Tre Scarperi** (1626m, **30min**). It stands on the side of a beautiful extended grassy basin, Campo di Dentro, surrounded by a forest of dwarf mountain pine that has colonised ancient scree flows. ▸

On path n.11, continue S on the level valley floor, where trees are gradually submerged by the ongoing river of scree. Ignore the first fork R (for Forcella Baranci) but take the second at the **junction** (1693m, **30min**), which is marked by a memorial to alpine soldiers. Well-graded path n.11 turns SW towards the Croda dei Rondoi rock barrier. At a junction (1895m) keep L (SSW) up a long series of steeper curves and scattered timbers left over from WW1.

Passo Grande dei Rondoi (2289m, **1hr 30min**), a narrow saddle that connects to Val Rienza, is a good excuse to get your breath back while you admire Rocca dei Baranci and Cima Piatta Bassa north. Phew!

Turn L to a rock face where a fixed cable and rungs give reassuring aid up a short chimney. Before you know it, you're up on a spectacular straightforward path SE, crossing the grassy slopes of Schwaben Alm and accompanied by a breathtaking panorama, the centrepiece of which are

Dominating the skyline northwest is the jagged Rocca dei Baranci, while due south Monte Mattina divides the valley in two.

the soaring Tre Cime. You bear E uphill, under Torre dei Scarperi, to a crest (2519m) dotted with WW1 constructions. A descent leads onto a flat pasture and **Passo Alpe Mattina** (2360m), home to marmots.

A final short uphill section leads NE past caverns to the head of a wide unnamed gully and the key **junction** (2431m, **45min**). Here, as path n.11 heads E towards the Torre di Toblin and landmark Rifugio Locatelli, you leave it to begin the return leg, turning sharp L (N) downhill to follow signposts for Rifugio Tre Scarperi. The long but problem-free descent path (n.105) passes through a sequence of troughs before an old wartime mule track takes over on the eastern flank of Monte Mattina. You cross a bridge in the proximity of what's left of a military goods lift, while vegetation reappears with mixed wood and alpenrose shrubs.

After around 700m in descent, you reach the vast scree-filled valley once again near a waterfall, and soon arrive back at the **junction** (1693m). From here, retrace your steps to **Rifugio Tre Scarperi** (**1hr 50min**) then back to the **Antoniusstein car park** (**25min**), where this magnificent route began.

WALK 7

The Val Fiscalina Tour

Start/Finish	Dolomitenhof, Pian di Val Fiscalina
Distance	17.8km
Ascent/Descent	1225m
Grade	2
Walking time	6hr
Map	Tabacco n.010 scale 1:25,000
Refreshments	Rifugio Fondo Valle, Rifugio Zsigmondy-Comici, Rifugio Pian di Cengia, Rifugio Locatelli
Access	A daily SAD bus connects Sesto via Moso to Pian di Val Fiscalina with the landmark Dolomitenhof hotel and car park where the motorable road ends.

Some of the most breathtaking and best-loved landscapes in the Dolomites are accessible on this superb round trip in the wonderful Sesto nature park, including the iconic Tre Cime. Meadows thick with wild flowers and picturesque alpine tarns give way to ever-changing scenery of spires and pinnacles, soaring peaks and vast scree slopes. During World War 1 a front line cut across the articulated mountain range, lines of trenches snaking their way along dividing ridges.

As attested by the high visitor numbers, there's something for everyone here, starting with lovely Val Fiscalina where a jingling horse-drawn cart, aka environmentally friendly taxi, rattles along as far as Rifugio Fondo Valle. Higher up is a string of high-altitude huts, each a wonderful place for refreshment or meals, unless you opt for a picnic.

As described here, this rewarding tour is long and tiring though not especially difficult. It can easily be split into two wonderful and more straightforward return routes to either Rifugio Zsigmondy-Comici (770m height gain/loss, 4hr return) or Rifugio Locatelli (950m height gain/loss, 4hr 30min return).

From the Dolomitenhof (1454m), a delightful level lane (n.102/103) heads due S in the shade of the mammoth Tre Scarperi. Ahead, the layout of the mountains dubbed the 'Sesto sun dial' becomes clear: southeast is Cima Dieci (ten o'clock peak), better known as Croda Rossa di Sesto, then south-southeast stands Cima Undici (eleven), due south (naturally) is Cima Dodici (twelve), also known as Croda dei Toni, while Cima Una (one) south-southwest overshadows the family-run eatery **Rifugio Fondo Valle** (1548m, **20min**).

Plough straight ahead past the hut on what quickly becomes a path across bleached gravel terrain anchored by spreading dwarf mountain pines. A pictorial signboard marks a strategic fork at the opening of Val Sassovecchio: go L on n.103 to ascend Val Fiscalina Alta. The ascent along the eastern flank of Cima Una is relentless, although there are welcome distractions in the form of alpenrose and marvellous views. Zigzags take the sting out of the steepest final sections to **Rifugio Zsigmondy-Comici** (2224m, **1hr 50min**), where you can collapse on the wonderful terrace and admire Croda dei Toni.

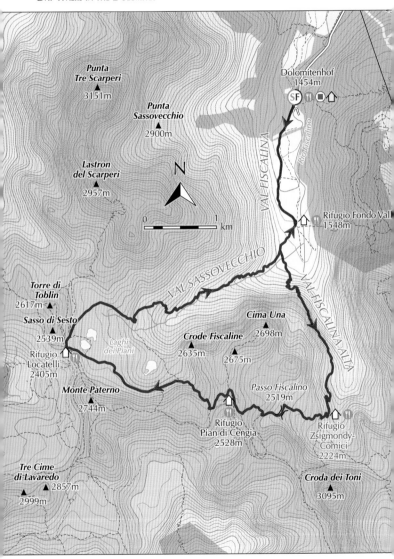

Across the valley to the east, a horizontal ledge can be seen below Monte Popera: during World War 1 it was hewn out of the rock face then painstakingly fitted with cables, coming to be known as the *Strada degli Alpini*. A popular aided route nowadays, it requires experience and gear; if you don't have either you can purchase one of the incredible postcards!

A further 300m climb is next on the agenda as path n.101 follows a winding wartime route W. Meagre patches of grass and hardy daisies are interspersed with stone and scattered war remains on the approach to the col, **Passo Fiscalino** (2519m). Leaving the Croda dei Toni behind you, keep R along the ample ledge for nearby **Rifugio Pian di Cengia** (2528m, **1hr**). ▶

Tucked into a sheltering rock alcove, this tiny hut serves delicious soups to hearten walkers in the windy chill that often prevails here.

The fantastic setting of Rifugio Locatelli

A shallow notch in the rock crest, **Forcella Pian di Cengia** (2522m) is the next landmark. It leads into an immense scree-filled amphitheatre littered with wartime timbers and barbed wire. On path n.101 you drop abruptly N via a barren gully before the path levels out for a panoramic traverse W, the stark surrounds enlivened by yellow Rhaetian poppies and lilac round-leaved pennycress. A sparkling emerald tarn lies below. The final section crosses welcome grassy terrain below **Monte Paterno** and the 'sausage' (Frankfurter Wurstel), and above the pretty cluster of the Laghi dei Piani.

Rifugio Locatelli (2405m, **1hr**) at Forcella di Toblin must be the most-visited hut in the whole of the Dolomites for its amazing position opposite the spectacular, world famous Tre Cime di Lavaredo. Their sheer flanks rise solemnly from an immense base of scree, and take on beautiful hues of pink and orange at sunset. The hut is also visited on Walk 8.

From here it's all downhill E on path n.102. You traverse a pasture basin, Alpe dei Piani, before things become a little steeper. Timber crossbars reinforce the path in an

The lovely Laghi dei Piani

effort to minimise the erosion caused by the thousands of boots that tread the route. You are soon in Val Sassovecchio, which runs between the impressive Crode Fiscaline and Cima Una, and the Tre Scarperi. The path sticks close to a meagre stream, the odd tree appearing above the scrubby shrubs. Keep L at the n.102/n.103 junction for the short, shady stretch to **Rifugio Fondo Valle** (1548m, **1hr 30min**), before returning to **Dolomitenhof** (**20min**).

WALK 8
The Tre Cime di Lavaredo Loop

Start/Finish	Rifugio Auronzo
Distance	9.8km (+1.5km for extension to Sasso di Sesto)
Ascent/Descent	450m (+135m for extension to Sasso di Sesto)
Grade	1–2
Walking time	3hr 30min (+40min for extension to Sasso di Sesto)
Map	Tabacco n.010 scale 1:25,000
Refreshments	Rifugio Auronzo, Rifugio Lavaredo, Rifugio Locatelli, Langalm
Access	From Misurina, a 7km toll road terminates at Rifugio Auronzo and a huge car park. Once it's full, the road is closed. However summer shuttle buses come up this far – Dolomiti Bus from Misurina, and SAD buses from Dobbiaco.

One of the most photographed landmarks of the Dolomites is the magnificent Tre Cime di Lavaredo (the Three Peaks, Drei Zinnen in German), likened to 'Egyptian Colossi' by Gilbert and Churchill (1864). Peaking at 2999m with the Cima Grande, they were not successfully scaled until 1896 by Paul Grohmann. An enduring magnet for ambitious climbers attracted by the magnificent sheer faces, which turn pastel pinks and all but flame red towards sundown, they are easily visited at close quarters by walkers.

This circumnavigation on foot is a wonderful way to admire the Tre Cime's unusual shapes – sharp points inexplicably transformed into soft corners, and the three distinct sections apparently merging into one. They are separated by profound cleft gashes caused by erosion along ancient fault lines. Good paths lead all the way round on open terrain with vast views.

A word on the area's popularity: it gets extremely busy in the summer months, so don't expect to have this spectacular walk to yourself. Take your own drink and food unless you plan on queuing up at the huts en route, and remember that you're at a fairly high altitude and should always carry protective clothing.

The Sesto Dolomites were involved in World War 1, and wherever you turn are poignant reminders; trenches gouged out of the rock, barricades of stones and barbed wire.

From Rifugio Auronzo (2320m) head E along the wide, level former military track n.101, beneath the awesome threesome, the Tre Cime. After a commemorative chapel, the way curves N to **Rifugio Lavaredo** (2344m) on a vast stony platform. Here, unless you prefer the steeper short cut L, stay with n.101 as it climbs gently to veer NW beneath Croda Passaporto to reach **Forcella Lavaredo** (2454m). Here another breathtaking panorama opens up: aside the lateral views onto the Tre Cime which defy description, you have the northern line-up of the Tre Scarperi and Baranci. This saddle was strategic during the hostilities, and it was from here that Rifugio Locatelli was shelled and burnt down in 1915. ◀

Wide path n.101 continues N, dipping below the ridge of Monte Paterno which is riddled with wartime tunnels. A lovely traverse cuts across dramatic scree slopes. At a signed fork, branch R for the short climb up an outcrop to **Rifugio Locatelli** (2405m, **1hr 30min**).

RIFUGIO LOCATELLI

Located at Forcella di Toblin, it is a stunning spot for admiring the northern face of the Tre Cime. First opened in 1883 at the cost of 813 florins, the hut needed extensions soon afterwards as visitor numbers in the following seven-year period shot up to 3375. The figure would barely cover a day now in midsummer! The hut also carries the name of Sepp Innerkofler, a famed local mountaineer, guide and former custodian. After he fell fighting on the Paterno under the Austro-Hungarian flag, as a sign of respect, the Italians gave him burial honours.

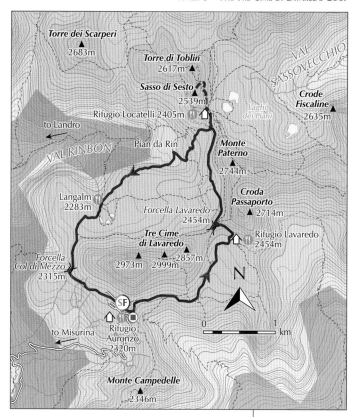

A recommended side trip follows to Sasso di Sesto, fiercely contested during World War 1.

Extension to Sasso di Sesto (40min return)
Behind the hut is the Sasso di Sesto, its base pierced by a line of man-made rock windows. A signed path for the Via Ferrata Torre di Toblin starts near the chapel. Follow this up to the saddle that separates the Torre di Toblin from the Sasso di Sesto, and turn sharp L (S) for the

The track leading across scree towards Rifugio Locatelli, backed by Sasso di Sesto

nearby 2539m top, an extraordinary lookout. Return the same way to Rifugio Locatelli.

Main route

The glorious return is marginally quieter than the outward route, and gives ample time to appreciate the colossal peaks. From **Rifugio Locatelli** either retrace your steps to the turn-off fork or take n.102, looping down below the hut in ample curves. Ignore turn-offs for Landro, but make sure you fork R (SW) on n.105. This drops easily through dwarf mountain pines and past colonies of shy marmots.

The spectacular threesome seen from the northwest

Stick with this well-trodden path and continue in decisive descent, bearing diagonally down timber steps into the sparsely grassed basin **Pian da Rin** (2180m). ▶ Then keep L for the steady ascent WSW, high above plunging **Val Rinbon**. Gaining a rise you find yourself within close range of the mighty threesome once more. Low-growing bushes accompany the way to farm-cum-café **Langalm** (2283m), a lovely spot to drink in yet more amazing views, and popular with choughs.

Early summer visitors can expect patches of snow in hollows here.

The ongoing path touches on a clutch of small but attractive tarns, during easy steady ascent which concludes at **Forcella Col di Mezzo** (2315m). This marks the return to the south side of the Tre Cime, with more wonderful views over the Cadini, Sorapiss and the Marmarole ranges. N.105 continues SE for the final strolling stretch back to **Rifugio Auronzo** (**2hr**).

WALK 9

Through the Cadini di Misurina

Start/Finish	Lago d'Antorno
Distance	8.5km
Ascent/Descent	580m
Grade	2+
Walking time	3hr 10min
Map	Tabacco n.010 scale 1:25,000
Refreshments	Lago d'Antorno, Rifugio Fonda Savio
Access	Lago d'Antorno is 2km from Misurina, reachable by Dolomiti Bus from Cortina or the SAD service from Dobbiaco. Car parking is available at the lake or at the start of the nearby track for Rifugio Fonda Savio.

The marvellous Cadini di Misurina are an awe-inspiring series of jagged crests, slender spires and a host of massive towers dissected by vast abrupt valleys and cirques – these are the actual *cadin* or *ciadin*, derived from 'rocky cirque' or valley, though the term has been extended to the mountains themselves. Crazy shapes rise from a pedestal of dark green forest and pasture. It is a playground for climbers, though luckily a number of excellent paths also lead walkers into the magical inner realms. The Cadini are rarely busy, in stark contrast with their close neighbour, the renowned Tre Cime di Lavaredo/Drei Zinnen group which draws great crowds.

The itinerary described here begins at a lovely lake with a café-restaurant and guesthouse. It embarks on a straightforward 550 metres uphill to Rifugio Fonda Savio. Immediately afterwards is a 50 metre descent down a rock face, aided by fixed cable. This is classified as a *sentiero attrezzato* aided route (in contrast to a more difficult full-blooded via ferrata climb). While not excessively exposed, it does require a sure foot and no vertigo. By all means take a look, then if it doesn't appeal simply turn back via the refuge the same way you came up. Remember that snow lies late well into summer in the sheltered valleys here.

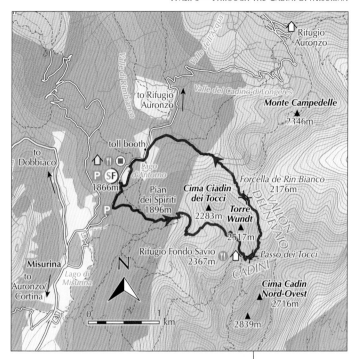

At Lago d'Antorno (1866m), take time out to admire Rifugio Fonda Savio, clearly visible at the head of an immense valley. Then leave the lake, walking down the road for half a kilometre to the start of a lane n.115 (1800m) forking L. Through thick wood only 10min up is the loading point for the hut's goods cableway at **Pian dei Spiriti** (1896m). Here a clear path takes over for the steady winding climb E up flowered flanks. At about 2100m you enter the vast scree valley of Ciadin dei Tocci, a magnificent amphitheatre surrounded by soaring peaks such as Punta dei Spiriti and Cima d'Antorno. ▶ A set of wooden stairs leads up to the rock platform and commanding position of **Rifugio Fonda Savio** (2367m, **1hr 30min**). It is dominated to the south by slender Torre

Above the tree line are masses of colourful wild flowers, such as Rhaetian poppies, pink thrift and mountain avens, though your attention will probably be set on *Torre Wundt* above.

79

The Tre Cime from Lago d'Antorno

If the ensuing aided stretch is not for you, return to Lago d'Antorno the way you came. If you do proceed, put trekking poles away to keep your hands free for the descent.

Alvise and Castello Incantato (enchanted castle) alongside Cima Cadin Nord-Ovest. The hut was built in 1963 by the Trieste CAI branch in memory of three brothers who lost their lives during World War 2, and is an exemplary, spotlessly clean hut run along traditional lines.

◀ From the building take n.117, Sentiero attrezzato Alberto Bonacossa, up to nearby **Passo dei Tocci** where it disappears over the edge L (NB: don't fork R for Forcella del Diavolo). Dropping diagonally down rock faces it is partially aided by cables and entails some hands-on clambering. After a matter of 10–15min, at the bottom, stick to the path straight ahead, ignoring the branch R (n.112). Proceed N down desolate and awesome Vallon del Nevaio. As the name suggests, snow persists well into summer here, covering the chaos of fallen rocks. The going is tiring, and you need to follow red/white waymarks carefully. The towering Tre Cime come into sight straight ahead. You coast around to **Forcella de Rin Bianco** (2176m, **40min**) and a series of World War 1 fortifications.

A steep gully descends into Vallon del Nevaio

Ignore the forks R and keep on n.119 signed for *casello pedaggio* (toll booth). It heads easily NW down the Ciadin de Rinbianco, with excellent views of Monte Piana and its zigzagging military tracks. A cluster of massive fallen boulders beneath the Cima Ciadin dei Tocci precedes entry into a stony gully. This descends to woodland and a lane. ▸

The Tre Cime are even more majestic from this angle.

Go L to approach the toll booth for the Rifugio Auronzo road. Without dropping to the roadside, stay on the clear path marked with yellow arrows, over a rise to the lakeside. To avoid the tarmac, keep L around the water's edge to where you began the walk at **Lago d'Antorno (1hr)**.

81

WALK 10

Monte Piana

Start/Finish	Lago d'Antorno (or Bar Genzianella for jeep shuttle)
Distance	14km (4.5km if jeep shuttle used)
Ascent/Descent	920m (230m if jeep shuttle used)
Grade	2+ (2 if aided stretches are avoided)
Walking time	4hr 30min (2hr 15min if jeep shuttle used)
Maps	Tabacco n.010 or n.03 scale 1:25,000
Refreshments	Lago d'Antorno, Rifugio Bosi
Access	Summer Dolomiti Bus runs from Misurina, SAD buses from Dobbiaco. From Bar Genzianella near Misurina a handy June–Oct jeep shuttle (tel 338 5282447 or 336 309730) ferries visitors up to Rifugio Bosi.

This walk will easily take up the best part of a day as the mountain top is honeycombed with networks of trenches, shelters, fortifications and tunnels which beg to be explored. And then there are the marvellous 360-degree panoramas – you'll make good use of the PeakFinder app.

Reasonable height gain and loss are entailed in the walk but this and the total time can be reduced thanks to the shuttle service.

MONTE PIANA

The Italians have justly baptised this mountain 'Monte Pianto' [Mountain of Tears]. It has already cost our side and the Italians so much blood and will cost even more, that I do not know if its possession can justify such a great sacrifice… So many have been buried here! So many corpses alongside the trenches! I'm not the one to say if this was really necessary; I only know that this is what was wanted by those in the rear, with their peremptory orders. In any case that's not my concern; my task is to obey.

Austrian army captain, World War 1

Monte Piana – a humble flat-topped mountain – stands only 12km from Val Pusteria, the heart of Südtirol defence during WW1. The northernmost part (Monte Piano) was an Austrian stronghold linked to Lago di Landro by two exposed paths and a mechanised cableway, while the southern knoll (Monte Piana) was Italian, supplied via a purpose-built mule track and a zigzagging road from what is now the modest resort of Misurina. The drawn-out hostilities, combined with terrible winters rife with devastating snow storms, caused shocking loss of life – 14,000 soldiers in total. The Italians abandoned the mountain in summer 1917, as reinforcements were urgently needed on the Isonzo front to the east.

A little earlier in history, Monte Piana was traversed by the border between the Republic of Venice and Austria, and granite marker stones dating back to 1753 are dotted over the plateau.

In the late 1970s an Austrian group, the Dolomitenfreunde, together with volunteers from all over Europe, set about creating an open-air museum with numbered landmarks. More info at www.montepiana.com.

The cross on Monte Piana and war caverns

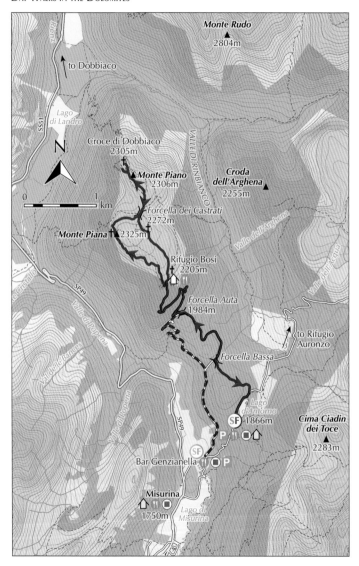

From the café-guesthouse at Lago d'Antorno (1866m), take the path alongside the road heading N. Just after the end of the lake, path n.122 forks off L (NW) through a wood of conifers interspersed with dwarf alpenrose. Not far in, at **Forcella Bassa**, you join a rough, partially surfaced lane used by the jeep shuttle. It climbs steadily and steeply in spots to reach **Forcella Auta** (1984m). Here you go R, joining the old WW1 military road, an especially panoramic route. ▶ Several short cuts are on hand.

Rifugio Bosi (2205m, **1hr 15min**) occupies a lovely scenic spot. To the L of the building, take n.122 NNW across the grassy slopes of the wind-swept plateau, devoid of tree cover. Some 10min on, fork L for the *Sentiero storico* (historic path). This quickly narrows to become a dramatic cliff-hugging route along the mountain's western edge, hundreds of dizzy metres above the valley floor. Short stretches of cable help around exposed corners. ▶

Weaving in and out of the folds of the mountain, the path links lookouts, tunnels and fortified positions, with gorgeous views west over to Monte Cristallo. From the prominent **cross** (landmark n.3) on **Monte Piana** (2325m) the blood-red flanks of Croda Rossa stand out. Here more goat-width paths dip under the cliffs to observation posts and caves. ▶

Now, criss-crossing deep trenches, make your way over to signs for landmarks n.6 then 5 and 7, a string of Italian wartime positions. Then head NE on a clear path cutting through low-lying dwarf mountain pines to a WW1 monument and **Forcella dei Castrati** (2272m). ▶

On path 6 proceed N towards the former Austrian-held plateau and Monte Piano. You touch on landmarks n.19 and 20, the dividing line with tunnels and trenches, and enjoy superb views to the iconic Tre Cime. Further along don't miss the brief detour L to n.22, a lookout, before the conclusion at the **Croce di Dobbiaco** (2305m, **1hr 30min**). This massive wooden cross stands on a remarkably dizzy viewpoint directly over Val di Landro and its lake. Underfoot is karstic paving, limestone rife with cracks and crevices – do watch your step.

The easy gradient gives you time to observe the magnificent Cristallo, Cadini and Tre Cime groups.

To avoid this exposed section, detour via the well-trodden path just back from the cliff top. It has no waymarking but is easy to follow to the cross on Monte Piana (see main route description).

Explore at will but watch your step.

This narrow rocky neck was no-man's land as it links two promontories occupied by opposing military forces. (An Italian mule track dropped R here to Val Rinbianco.)

Return to **Forcella dei Castrati** (2272m) and proceed straight ahead in the direction of Rifugio Bosi. However not far up branch L in ascent to a commemorative cross then head SSE to landmarks n.14/15/12, a maze of war-time positions – and mountain views. Keep L in descent alongside – or in – the trenches to former troop barracks, n.17. Then fork R (S) on the clear path looking over to the spiky Cadini. A shallow gully concludes at a cannon and chapel, only a flight of steps above **Rifugio Bosi** (2205m, **45min**).

If you're not tempted by the jeep shuttle down to Bar Genzianella, walk back the same way you came to **Lago d'Antorno** (**1hr**).

WALK 11
Lago di Misurina

Start/Finish	Grand Hotel Misurina bus stop
Distance	3km
Ascent/Descent	negligible
Grade	1
Walking time	1hr
Map	Tabacco n.03 scale 1:25,000
Refreshments	café-restaurants around the lake
Access	Misurina can be reached by Dolomiti Bus, which runs from Cortina and Auronzo as well as SAD from Dobbiaco. Car parking is plentiful.

Superbly photogenic Lago di Misurina vies with Braies and Carezza for the title 'most beautiful lake in the Dolomites'. Its deep blue-green transparent waters reflect a magnificent set of landmark mountains – starting with the Tre Cime di Lavaredo and the Sorapiss.

This relaxing stroll through shady woodland around the water's edge in the company of waterfowl, is a must-do. There are pedalo and rowing boat rentals should you be tempted by a spin over the water.

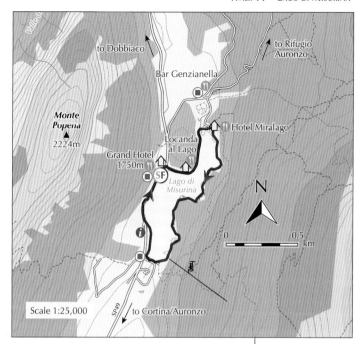

From the Grand Hotel Misurina bus stop (1750m) facing the lake, go L to follow the water's edge past Locanda al Lago and its terrace. Now you're on a quiet lane, heading for the northernmost extremity of the lake where thick beds of greenery are appreciated by the coots that thrive here. The way curves past a playground around to **Hotel Miralago**, beautifully situated with an inviting café platform for admiring the magnificent Sorapiss.

Here a clear path sets out to hug the water's edge, giving you time to enjoy the clear water where trout swim. Handy benches shaded by trees dot the way, looking out to a handful of tiny islands. The shore line ducks in and out, leading to the far end and a **chairlift** (Seggiovia Col de Varda). Go R past a monumental yellow building (a renowned clinic for respiratory problems). As you reach

87

With a view to the Sorapiss, Lago di Misurina is one of the most beautiful in the Dolomites

the road, turn R again near a bus stop and take the path parallel to the tarmac (lined with hotels and café-restaurants). This leads along the lake edge with a pedalo rental and picnic tables, without forgetting superb views and reflections of the Tre Cime and the Cadini.

Further along, a timber walkway takes you through to the **bus stop** at the Grand **Hotel Misurina** (**1hr**), a satisfying conclusion.

LAGO DI MISURINA

A legend explains its origin. Misurina was originally the name of the daughter of peace-loving king Sorapiss. The capricious girl ardently desired a magical mirror possessed by a witch, who in exchange wanted shade for her house. So the indulgent father obligingly transformed himself into a mighty rugged mountain. At a considerably later date, when she understood the weight of his sacrifice, Misurina wept tears of regret so copious as to form the lake, which reflects the massive shape of her petrified father.

In winter the lake freezes over and becomes a playing field for ice polo matches, during which the horses wear special crampons to stop them slipping.

WALK 12
Val Popena Alta

Start/Finish	Misurina tourist office
Distance	7km
Ascent/Descent	600m
Grade	2–3
Walking time	2hr 30min
Map	Tabacco n.03 scale 1:25,000
Refreshments	Misurina
Access	Misurina is served by summer buses from Cortina, Auronzo (Dolomiti Bus) and Dobbiaco (SAD).

This excellent loop walk starts on the banks of the famous Misurina lake (see Walk 11 for more info). A panoramic traverse leads to a steep section with loose rocks where a sure foot is needed. Timber steps and walkways lead up a rubble-choked gully to conclude on the lip of beautiful Val Popena, an especially quiet side valley that slots into the easternmost extremity of the Cristallo massif. Here stands a long abandoned, photogenic refuge in a spectacularly scenic location. Thereafter comes a narrow path traverse leading to a pass from where you loop down back to Misurina.

On the western bank of the lake at Misurina (1750m), between the tourist office and Hotel Lavaredo, follow signs for path n.224. W at first, head straight up over pastureland appreciated by cows, and into light wood. As you pass close to the dairy farm **Malga Misurina**, ignore the fork R for n.224a and keep on the old military track with its perfect gradient. ▸ The gradient steepens a little as broad curves lead toward the barrier of the Pale di Misurina. At a **fork** (1990m) you part ways with n.224 (the return route), and keep L on narrower n.224b (signed for the Rifugio Popera ruins (*ruderi*). The sun-beaten way leads SW through a sea of dwarf mountain pine and across bright white scree flows. ▸

The views back to the Tre Cime and the Cadini, not to mention the lake and the mighty Sorapiss, are inspiring.

It offers vast panoramas including the Val Ansiei's dark cloak of forest, which acts as a skirt to the Marmarole above.

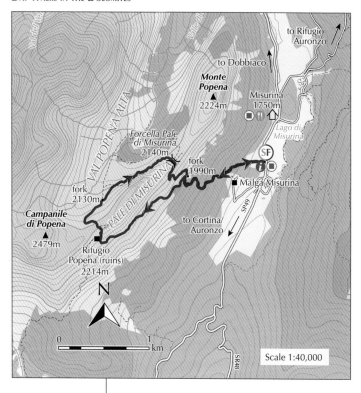

Soon after a Parco Dolomiti D'Ampezzo sign comes a sharp veer R. Now the path becomes near-vertical – watch your step. Up at a rock face you quickly find yourself on sturdy timber steps and dizzy walkways leading up the right side of an eroding rock-choked gully. It will be with relief that you emerge at Forcella di Popena and the grassy flat close to the ruins of **Rifugio Popena** (2214m, **1hr 15min**) at the head of awesome Val Popena Alta. ◀

This breathtaking spot looks to Piz Popena and a host of Sesto Dolomites.

Clear path n.222 curves downhill, affording a lovely angle onto the Campanile di Popena rock tower which bears a curious resemblance to the headgear traditionally

A view back down the timber steps and walkways leading up to Forcella di Popena

worn by Venetian doges. Down at a **fork** (2130m) leave the main path and go R on the clear if unnumbered path pointing NE. Marked with red dots it entails minor ups and downs and the odd narrow eroded bit beneath a towering ridge before you climb out at **Forcella Pale di Misurina** (2140m, **30min**). ▶

After getting your breath back, take n.224 in gentle descent to the **fork** (1990m) encountered on the way up. Branch L as per the ascent route back to the **Misurina tourist office** and lakefront (**45min**).

Stone walls bear witness to the WW1 activity here.

WALK 13
Rifugio Vandelli Traverse

Start/Finish	Passo Tre Croci
Distance	12.5km
Ascent/Descent	800m
Grade	2–3 (Grade 2 to and from Rifugio Vandelli)
Walking time	5hr (4hr to and from Rifugio Vandelli)
Map	Tabacco n.03 scale 1:25,000
Refreshments	Passo Tre Croci, Rifugio Vandelli
Access	Dolomiti Bus services link the Passo Tre Croci road pass with Cortina and Misurina throughout summer. Car drivers note: parking at the pass can be all but impossible.

In contrast to the rugged rocky heart of the Sorapiss, which soars to 3205m over the town of Cortina, the northernmost edge of the group is, luckily, accessible to the average walker. This rewarding and varied loop route leads to beautifully located Rifugio Vandelli on photogenic Lago di Sorapiss. And there are treats for geology buffs, with fossils en route. Be aware that the path as far as the refuge is extremely popular, though the ensuing higher traverse is more peaceful with a preponderance of animals such as chamois over two-footed visitors, combined with breathtaking views over neighbouring Dolomites.

The walk can be simplified if you limit yourself to the refuge and lake, a very satisfying route in itself, then return to the road pass the same way. Those who embark on the traverse (Grade 3 difficulty) should do so only in the best of weather as it reaches altitudes of over 2300m and involves exposed stretches as well as steep terrain with loose stones.

Not far E of Passo Tre Croci (1805m), you come to the start of a former military mule track, signed n.215. Going SE initially, it heads into the wood and spells level walking at first at the base of the Loudo and Marcoira (or Marcuoira) mountains, and passes several overgrown

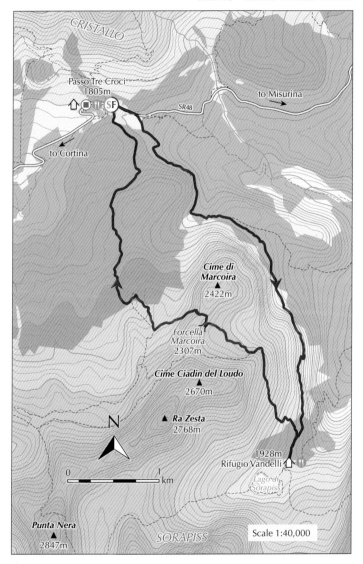

Ahead southeast is the rugged Marmarole range, and you glimpse the waterfall mentioned below.

forts. ◄ On the edge of a steep-sided valley the path turns upwards for the first of a series of metal ladders, straight-forward passages without notable exposure. As the path resumes its southern direction, the wood opens up and there's a longish narrow stretch aided by a guiding cable, but nothing too difficult.

With the gain in altitude, the tree cover is springy dwarf mountain pine for the most part, interspersed with larch. Keep your eyes on the ground, as a fascinating fossil zone is encountered: the dark soil underfoot alternates with white rock embedded with surprising numbers of heart-shaped outlines of Megalodonts, bivalve shells averaging 10cm in length from around 200 million years ago. ◄

They were once believed to be the hoofprints of the devil!

The name for the Sorapiss (or Sorapis) mountain is dialect for 'above the waterfall'. But according to legend, he was a king – (see Walk 11).

Modest **Rifugio Vandelli** (1928m, **2hr**) is not far up, occupying a wonderful position that looks out north to the Cadini and the Sesto Dolomites in the distance. Most visitors head straight to nearby **Lago di Sorapiss**; its unusually translucent green-blue water owes its milky appearance to suspended powdered debris from the three shrinking frontal glaciers on the awe-inspiring north-facing wall of Punta Sorapiss, the grandiose backdrop. ◄ Directly above the lake is the rocky point curiously referred to as Dito di Dio (finger of God).

RIFUGIO VANDELLI

Landmark Rifugio Vandelli has a chequered history to say the least. Originally constructed in 1891 by the Pfalzgau branch of the Austro-German Alpine Club, it has been repeatedly devasted by avalanches, rockfalls and even fire but painstakingly rebuilt on each occasion by its owners, now the Venice branch of CAI who took over after WW1 with the area's transfer to Italy.

Among the thinning trees and dwarf pines the chances increase of spotting fawn-coated chamois.

Backtrack on path n.215 downhill for about 10min from Rifugio Vandelli, and then branch L (NW) on n.216 heading decidedly uphill in zigzags towards the Cime Ciadin del Loudo. ◄ After an hour of steady ascent, a short aided stretch leads to a cable along a ledge (2243m) with astounding views and a little exposure. As this

finishes you enter the beautiful grassy basin of Ciadin del Loudo. Ignore the fork L (often closed for rockfalls) and keep straight ahead NW on n.216 up to the crest and panoramic **Forcella Marcoira** (2307m, **1hr 30min**).

Now watch your step as the path plunges over scree and loose rocks for a good 200 metres. The majestic Cristallo with its twin points stands out north. Finally down among grass and trees, at a junction you pick up path n.213 (R) for a leisurely descent on a forestry track N in shady woodland. This concludes at **Passo Tre Croci** (**1hr 30min**).

The spectacular aided ledge to Ciadin del Loudo

WALK 14

*Forcella Zumèles and
the Cristallo*

Start/Finish	Rio Gere
Distance	9.6km
Ascent/Descent	550m
Grade	2+
Walking time	3hr 15min
Map	Tabacco n.03 scale 1:25,000
Refreshments	Rio Gere, Brites de Larieto, Rifugio Mietres, Rifugio Son Forca (off-route)
Access	The summer time Dolomiti Bus between Cortina and Misurina stops at Rio Gere where there's ample car parking.

This loop route has wonderfully varied landscapes. It begins with a delightful ramble through an extensive larch forest. Then comes a stiff steep 300m ascent – which is not a Sunday stroll – leading to a renowned lookout and close-ups of the awesome Cristallo massif and its layered rock beds of geological fascination. An especially rewarding outing, though not for beginners and not in uncertain weather.

The walk start, Rio Gere, doubles as the departure station for a scenic chairlift ride up to Rifugio Son Forca at the base of the Cristallo – a half-hour uphill detour; if desired this could be used for as an alternative descent.

From Rio Gere (1680m) walk down the road below the chairlift and across a river of gravel. Fork R up to a crucifix and path junction where you branch L (W) on n.211. The clear path heads through larch trees to a farm-cum-café **Brites de Larieto** (1660m). Turn R (NW) on the gravel lane (still n.211) for a gentle uphill stretch. Further on is a 5min detour L for eatery Rifugio Mietres; ignore it unless you need food and proceed N on to the **Pousa de Zumèles** (1724m) junction. Here you leave the lane and

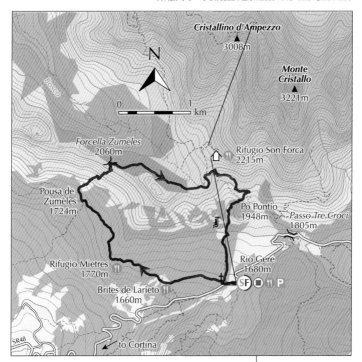

branch R on n.204, labelled for 'experts' due to the steep nature of the terrain.

Through clumps of dwarf mountain pines, the path climbs decidedly, zigzagging steeply NE up to follow a grassy shoulder studded with edelweiss. Then it enters a short shallow gully, problem-free thanks to timber path reinforcements. You emerge at the ridge-top and the pass **Forcella Zumèles** (2060m, **1hr 45min**). Once you've got your breath back you can start drinking in the views of the Cortina basin from the Pelmo to the Tofane and the Pomagagnon, and taking in the star of the day, the Cristallo close at hand.

Go R on n.205 past a WW1 tunnel. The way coasts mostly E as a wide track with stone edging, hinting at its

The path affords an impressive view up a gully on the Cristallo

There's an impressive view up a dramatic gully on the Cristallo.

military origin. ◄ You slot into a gravel lane, and keep R for a short distance. At a ski piste, leave the lane for signed path n.203. This leads R via a surprising spectacular gully where erosion has exposed the bright red rock beds underlying the main dolomite. Stay with the path under the chairlift, crossing a couple of streams and keeping high above the ski piste. ◄

The Sorapiss mountain can be admired ahead.

Finally down at a lane, turn R to the nearby clutch of signposts (**Po Pontio**, 1948m). Here you need path n.206 which plunges SW into the wood. It can be slippery going so watch your step. After crossing a stream you go under the chairlift again and up to a lane. Not far downhill is the clearing Pian de Fedèra (1790m) – leave n.206 now and walk straight ahead for Rio Gere. Past water troughs keep R downhill and keep your eyes peeled for red/white markers on trees. These show a clear path S that emerges from the forest at the crucifix and junction encountered at the walk start. Keep L to return to **Rio Gere** (**1hr 30min**).

WALK 15

Below the Antelao

Start/Finish	*Centro* bus stop, San Vito di Cadore
Distance	17.5km
Ascent/Descent	1200m
Grade	2
Walking time	5hr 30min (can be cut to 3hr 20min by starting from Rifugio Scotter or 4hr 50min from Baita Sun Bar)
Map	Tabacco n.025 scale 1:25,000
Refreshments	Rifugio Scotter, Rifugio San Marco, Rifugio Galassi
Access	The *centro* bus stop at San Vito, close to the main churches, is used by Dolomiti Bus, Cortina Express and ATVO. To shorten the ascent to Rifugio Scotter, by all means avail yourself of the *navetta* shuttle bus from Baita Sun Bar or slightly further up, the chair lift. (Check with the tourist office as to which is operating tel 0436 9238.) By car, park at Baita Sun Bar.

The walk heads out of the resort town of San Vito di Cadore, up through woods and modest ski areas, before a stiffish climb to the superb perch of an alpine hut perched on the edge of the rugged Marmarole and with brilliant Dolomite views. A narrow scree traverse leads to a pass with an excellent outlook at the foot of the majestic Antelao before plunging back to the start.

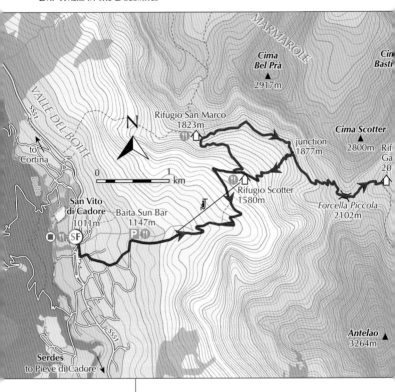

The majestic Pelmo can be admired from here across the valley.

From the *centro* bus stop at San Vito (1011m) follow 'ski area' signs leading initially S then bearing E across the old railway line/cycle track to pick up Via Belvedere, and proceed NE up to the winter ski area. Past Hotel Barancio is **Baita Sun Bar** (1147m, 20min). If you don't avail yourself of the shuttle bus or the chairlift a short way up, proceed on the forestry lane and ski pistes winding gently up to well positioned **Rifugio Scotter** (1580m, **50min**). ◀

Ignore path n.228 (unless you have a penchant for super steep puff-inducing paths) and stick with the wide track climbing above the building. At a sharp bend L is the junction with n.229 (the return route) but you stick

with n.226 steadily NW. It narrows to a path through trees, on the last leg of its climb to **Rifugio San Marco** (1823m, **1hr**), a marvellous family-run eyrie looking southeast to king Antelao.

After Rifugio San Marco the route crosses veritable rivers of scree

Now you need narrow n.227 that sets out E across awesome scree slopes where walkers are mere dots. The slope below Cima Bel Prà is subject to ongoing erosion and the path climbs in and out of channels gouged by water and rockfalls. Follow the red/white paint splashes carefully. About half an hour across, a **junction** (1877m) at a rock face marks the start of the descent for path n.229 (the return route) but it's well worth pushing on. The going becomes decidedly easier with gentle ascent, and low-lying plants have colonised the slopes.

Forcella Piccola (2102m, **1hr**) is a must for the views along the western flank of the Marmarole, not to mention over the Valle del Boite with the throne-like Pelmo and even the Tofane beyond Cortina. ◄

A fault line dividing the Dolomite rock of the Marmarole from the limestone of the Antelao, the pass is also a favourite hangout for ibex.

Down the other side, the simple stone building **Rifugio Galassi** (2018m, **10min**), formerly military barracks, occupies a spectacular position. It faces soaring Cima Scotter and looks over a tongue of ice from one of the Antelao's shrinking glaciers.

Return to **Forcella Piccola** and retrace your steps as far as the **junction** (1877m) where n.229 forks sharp L. Watch your step as this plunges madly in tight zigzags W, the way shown by red/white markers and cairns. Knee-challenged, you're back at **Rifugio Scotter** (**1hr 10min**) and need to return to **Baita Sun Bar** then **San Vito di Cadore** (**1hr**).

MYTHS OF THE MARMAROLE

The star of this walk is the pyramidal Antelao. According to an endearing story, the massive mountain is really the petrified body of a good-natured giant. His undoing was to fall in love – and ignite the ire of a jealous wicked witch. Her powerful curse turned him into stone and he pitched headlong into the valley, his heart a glacier the icy-blue colour of forget-me-not flowers.

The Marmarole range on the other hand has long been renowned for fearful avalanches and ongoing rockslides hurtling downhill, many a village irretrievably engulfed by deadly rivers of stone. Rumour has it these catastrophes are the work of the spiteful Croderes, mythical creatures who reside in ice palaces among the dizzy snowbound peaks. One of the most recent incidents put a chairlift out of action, played havoc with paths, and still keeps the maintenance crews on their toes as creeping scree threatens the main road.

WALK 16

Rifugio Padova and
Rifugio Tita Barba

Start/Finish	Car park near Rifugio Padova
Distance	12km
Ascent/Descent	950m
Grade	2
Walking time	5hr 15min
Map	Tabacco n.016 scale 1:25,000
Refreshments	Rifugio Padova, Rifugio Tita Barba
Access	From Domegge di Cadore turn SE for the road across the Lago di Centro Cadore. It narrows for the 8.5km climb to the car park near Rifugio Padova. Time restrictions apply in summer for traffic – check the refuge web site. Public transport (Dolomiti Bus) is only useful as far as Domegge then you'll need a taxi (tel 330 241982).

This is a glorious, if lengthy, foray into the beautiful, peaceful reaches of the Spalti di Toro-Monfalconi, one of the rugged Dolomite ranges in the far eastern sector of the Cadore, and well off the mainstream tourist track. Thick and often impenetrable conifer forest clothes the valleys right up to the reign of rock and scree, providing shelter for elusive deer and squirrels, although the many clearings for woodcutters and summer farms afford sweeping views of the group's magnificent spires and towers. In the 1860s, Gilbert and Churchill ventured as far as Casera Vedorcia and counted a total of 30 rocky points and spires belonging to the Spalti–Monfalconi.

Apart from several steepish tracts, this brilliant loop route amounts to a walk of average difficulty, well worth it in early summer for the abundance of unusual wild flowers such as the lady's slipper orchid, not to mention autumn for the golden colours. The two hospitable refuges can provide both delicious meals and accommodation but for a picnic buy supplies in Domegge beforehand.

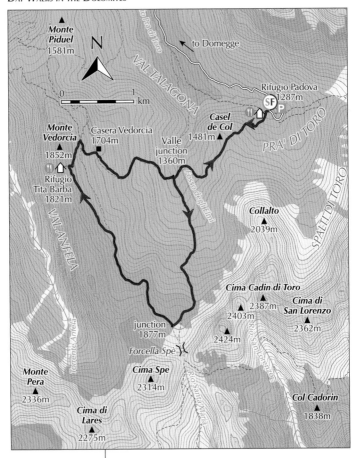

Set on the lower edge of the Pra' di Toro (Thor's meadows), it faces the magnificent spread of the Spalti di Toro-Monfalconi rock spires.

Picturesque and homely Rifugio Padova is a matter of minutes from the car park. ◄

Accompanied by all manner of marvellous sculptured figures, path n.350/352 makes its way SW, mostly through thick conifer forest, climbing and winding round Collalto. A lengthy descent leads along and across a series of streams with lovely pools and cascades.

Not far on you reach a hut and the **Valle junction** (1360m, **1hr**), where the return route links back in. Now break off L (S) on n.352. A clear but constantly steep path, it initially climbs alongside the watercourse Fosso degli Elmi. The trees thin to give way to a clamber up a narrow gully, which concludes as you emerge onto a veritable river of bleach-white scree. This is dotted with pretty clumps of lilac pennycress and edged by larch and dwarf pines, in a magnificent amphitheatre of soaring peaks and turrets, the wondrous Spalti di Toro.

A short distance below **Forcella Spè**, visible above, you come to a wider path at another **junction** (1877m, **1hr 30min**).

Branch R on n.350 for a leisurely panoramic traverse NW. It concludes at **Rifugio Tita Barba** (**45min**) on Monte Vedorcia. Standing in a picturesque flowered clearing, this idyllic Hansel and Gretel house (built by a local enthusiast in the 1930s, and still run by the family) offers basic amenities and hearty local dishes. ▶

On the far side a path leads over to a marvellous lookout towards the Marmarole, Antelao and Pelmo.

Rifugio Padova occupies a beautiful spot

Vast and inspiring views take in Monte Cridola and the Spalti di Toro-Monfalconi, as well as the isolated tower Campanile di Val Montanaia. ◄

Take the jeep track NNE dropping across a rough lane before veering SE and ducking in and out between timber chalets. The path (still n.350) leads past magnificent meadows and the sprawling summer dairy farm **Casera Vedorcia**. ◄

Resume the clear path in descent, particularly steep on this stretch, back to the **Valle junction** (1360m, **1hr**) encountered earlier. Go straight ahead to return to **Rifugio Padova** and the car park the same way you came earlier (**1hr**).

WALK 17
The Pramper Circuit

Start/Finish	Pian de la Fopa, Val Pramper
Distance	13.5km
Ascent/Descent	750m
Grade	1–2
Walking time	4hr 15min
Map	Tabacco n.025 scale 1:25,000
Refreshments	Malga Pramper, Rifugio Pramperet
Access	Dolomiti Bus has year-round connections to Forno di Zoldo. Here, a summer jeep shuttle service (tel 348 6700786 www.zoldobus.it) runs up to Pian de la Fopa (5km) and Malga di Pramper (4km). Private traffic is permitted as far as the Pian de la Fopa car park.

Branching south off the Val di Zoldo, a mere crow's flight from the landmarks Pelmo and Civetta, quiet Val Pramper lies in the realms of the Dolomiti Bellunesi National Park. Bound by minor but memorable mountains and clad in thick conifer woods, with the occasional clearing used for pastoral purposes, it is well worth exploring. The Spiz di Mezzodì group for example has countless weird and wonderful spires, high above remarkable rivers of scree, some of the most extensive in the whole of the Dolomites. Val Pramper receives far fewer visitors than its more famous neighbours – despite the fact that the long-distance Alta Via 1 transits in the upper part – and abounds in animal life and wonderful wild flowers.

This straightforward loop route follows both wide tracks and clearly marked paths. At around 2000m altitude, the central traverse is a guarantee of magnificent views.

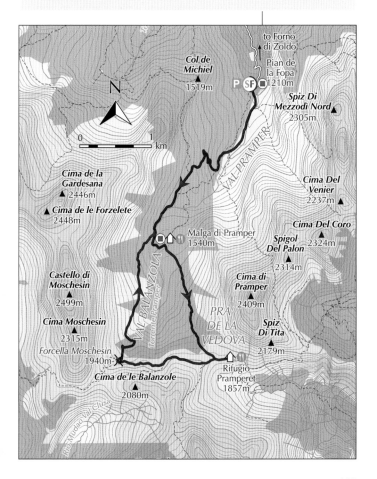

From the car park at Pian de la Fopa (1210m), the rough road (n.523) continues SW in conifer wood parallel to the stream. As the track veers W at the foot of the rambling San Sebastiano group, an optional old path cuts the corner, rejoining on aptly named Pian dei Palui (plain of the marshes) rich in aquatic plants and grasses. The fork for n.540, the return route, is not far further up, but stick to the track for the time being to reach nearby **Malga di Pramper** (1540m, **1hr**). Set in an ancient glacial basin, this working summer farm-cum-eatery has overnight options.

From here path n.523 proceeds SSE, ascending steeply at times, at the foot of imposing Cima di Pramper. After a shrine on a rise (1753m), you come to the lush pasture of **Pra' de la Vedova** (the widow's meadow), which owes its fertility to an underlying stratum of clay that holds in moisture. It is strewn with chunks of rock that have detached themselves from neighbouring mountains.

On the panoramic path towards Forcella Moschesin

Rifugio Pramperet (1857m, **1hr**) is an ensemble of timber and stone huts overlooking a deep valley in front

of the wild Cime de Zita and Talvena. The staff cook up delicious local dishes such as spicy Pastin sausage served with polenta.

In common initially with Alta Via 1, you strike out through thickets of springy dwarf mountain pines heading due W on n.543 – take care not to inadvertently branch L in ascent for Forcella di Zita. Clearings dotted with larch are home to masses of martagon lilies, while you enjoy stunning views of the Pelmo, due north, rising throne-like above a sea of conifers. Follow signs up over rock below Cima de le Balanzole, before a short drop to **Forcella Moschesin** (1940m, **45min**). ▶

For the descent, turn sharp R (NE) on n.540 to head in wide curves down Val Balanzola under the Castello di Moschesin, an offshoot of the Tamer group. This rejoins the ascent track a stone's throw from **Malga di Pramper**, and from there you need to take the rough road once more to return to **Pian de la Fopa** (**1hr 30min**).

The ample saddle has alpenrose shrubs and bellflowers as well as shelters and tunnel systems dating back to WW1, and a ruined stone barracks.

WALK 18
Lago Coldai and the Civetta

Start	Alleghe gondola lifts
Finish	Listolade
Distance	20.5km
Ascent	800m
Descent	2040m
Grade	2
Walking time	7hr (3hr 30min if limited to Forcella Col Negro; 6hr if using taxi to Listolade/Alleghe)
Maps	Tabacco n.015 or n.025 scale 1:25,000
Refreshments	Piani di Pezzè, Col dei Baldi, Rifugio Coldai, Rifugio Tissi, Rifugio Vazzoler, Rifugio Capanna Trieste
Access	Both Alleghe and Listolade are served by year-round Dolomiti Bus. From Alleghe, gondola lifts run via Piani di Pezzè to Col dei Baldi. Towards walk's end a taxi can be booked to save 1hr.

The grand façade of the Civetta – a sheer, magnificent wall of upright precipice, seamed from crown to foot with thousands of vertical fissures, and rising in a mighty arch towards the centre – faces to the north-west, looking directly up the Cordevole towards Caprile, and filling the end of the valley as a great organ-front fills in the end of a Cathedral aisle.

Amelia Edwards (1873)

This extremely rewarding if demanding full-day traverse follows a section of the renowned Alta Via 1, along the base of the Civetta's superb and unequalled northwestern face. The 3220m phenomenal trident-shaped Dolomite was first scaled in 1867 by the English climber Francis Fox Tuckett. The name actually means 'owl' in Italian, derived from local dialect. Awe-inspiring scenery is the flavour of the day with lakes, masses of flowered pasture slopes and shady woods alive with animal life, not to mention a string of hospitable mountain huts, which make marvellous rest and refreshment stops. They also offer overnight accommodation for anyone who prefers to spread the walk over two days, instead of squeezing it into one. On the contrary you can easily shorten the walk to 3hr 30min (return) by visiting Lago Coldai then going a tad further to Forcella Col Negro, where the Civetta's organ-front is revealed in all its glory, before returning the way you came.

The walk start Alleghe is a modest lakeside mountain resort that lies in the Civetta's imposing shadow. In addition to an ice rink, it boasts gondola lifts essential to reaching the walk's start.

Set beneath Monte Coldai, it looks across to the magnificent Pelmo, as well as a host of minor Dolomites.

After the leisurely ascent by lifts from Alleghe (978m) via Piani di Pezzè (1470m) to **Col dei Baldi** (1922m, **15min**) and its café-restaurants, turn R (SE) in descent on a white gravel track. A short stroll downhill is former dairy farm **Malga Pioda** (1816m). Here, in common with AV1, broad path n.556/564 aka a wartime mule track makes its way SSW in slow zigzags, which take the sting out of the steep climb. At times it hugs the cliff face, a veritable rock garden. Just after the hut's goods cableway stands welcoming **Rifugio Coldai** (2132m, **1hr 15min**). ◄

From the end of the sun terrace, well-trodden path n.560 climbs steeply due W to a wide neck, Forcella Coldai (2191m), offering views of the Marmolada. It's

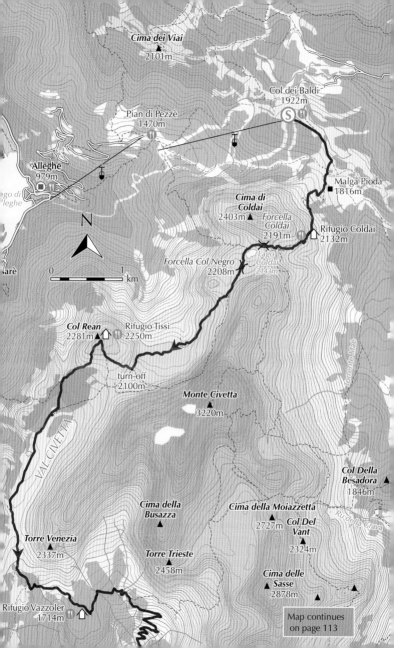

Cima dei Viai
2101m

Col. dei Baldi
1922m

Pian di Pezzè
1470m

Alleghe
979m

_go di_
eghe

Malga Pioda
1816m

Cima di Coldai
2403m

Forcella Coldai
2191m

Rifugio Coldai
2132m

Forcella Col Negro
2208m

Lago Coldai
2143m

N

0   1 km

Col Rean
2281m

Rifugio Tissi
2250m

turn-off
2100m

Monte Civetta
3220m

sarè

VAL CIVETTA

Col Della Besadora
1846m

Cima della Busazza

Cima della Moiazzetta
2727m

Col Del Vant
2324m

Ru della Grava

Torrente Maè

Torre Venezia
2337m

Torre Trieste
2458m

Cima delle Sasse
2878m

Rifugio Vazzoler
1714m

Map continues
on page 113

Lovely Lago Coldai is a rewarding destination

To shorten the route to 3hr 30min, retrace your steps to return to Col dei Baldi and the lifts back to Alleghe.

If time is tight, skip Rifugio Tissi by continuing straight on into Val Civetta.

only a short drop to the shallow cirque housing milky-green **Lago Coldai** (2143m); its sandy shore and grassy surrounds are great for picnics, a fact exploited by the flocks of yellow-beaked choughs that appear out of nowhere at the rustling of a food wrapper.

After looping round the tarn the path climbs S to **Forcella Col Negro** (2208m, **30min**) where the marvellous elongated western face of the Civetta comes into view in all its glory, the 'wall of walls' which rises some 1200m from the scree base to a maximum of 3220m. ◄ The next stretch is easily the most spectacular of the day. Ignore the tempting high scree variant, both tricky and dangerous, and stick to the official route that drops 100m through a stony grass basin before re-ascending to the turn-off (2100m, **1hr**) below Col Rean. Here, fork R uphill. ◄

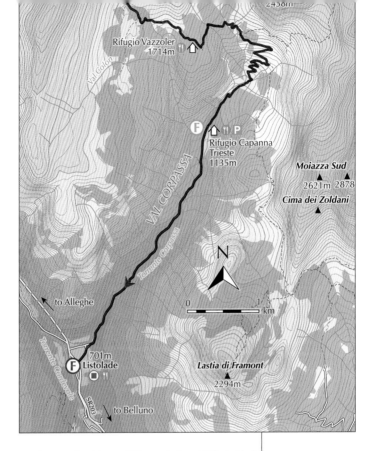

A steep slog N on n.563 concludes at **Rifugio Tissi**
(**30min**), lookout par excellence for the Civetta, the
mountain's 'eye' or trademark pocket glacier, the Giazer,
hanging onto the sheer rock. The cross above the building
affords a dizzying view of the plunge to Alleghe and vast
views of the San Martino group, Marmolada, Sella and
others beyond.

Without returning to the turn-off (2100m), head SW
on path n.560 into Val Civetta where it crosses undulating pasture basins and dodges boulders. Gentle descent
rounds the foot of magnificent Torre Venezia, renowned

Torre Venezia soars above the path to Rifugio Vazzoler

A further attraction is the well-kept alpine flower rock garden.

for its climbing routes. You join a rough farm track for the final dusty stretch SE, to where **Rifugio Vazzoler** (1714m, **1hr 30min**) nestles in a wood of delicate larch trees. The impeccable old-style hut makes for a wonderful stopover, its picnic tables looking onto sheer ochre-tinted Torre Trieste and the imposing spread of the Moiazza group. ◄

Jeep track n.555 resumes E, zigzagging easily downhill through spreads of dwarf mountain pines and across streams. You can see all the way down Val Corpassa to the cluster of houses at Listolade, backed by Monte Agner.

At **Rifugio Capanna Trieste** (1135m, **1hr**), ▶ the track becomes a narrow surfaced road for a straightforward stroll to **Listolade** (**1hr**) in Val Cordevole and the SS203, where you can take the bus back to **Alleghe**.

To save 1hr, book a taxi to take you from Rifugio Capanna Trieste to Listolade and on to Alleghe. Tel 348 5658675 or 340 6796016.

WALK 19
The Pelmo Tour

Start/Finish	Passo Staulanza
Distance	13.5km (5km for short route)
Ascent/Descent	1100m (330m for short route)
Grade	3 (2 for short route)
Walking time	6hr (+30min detour to fossils) (2hr 30min for short route)
Map	Tabacco n.015 scale 1:25,000
Refreshments	Passo Staulanza, Rifugio Venezia
Access	A summer Dolomiti Bus stops at the road pass at the head of Val di Zoldo.

This is a circumnavigation of one of the most impressive Dolomites, the 3168m Pelmo.

This memorable walk can be completed in a single day with good weather, but you need to make an early start. Other requisites are a sure foot, plenty of puff, and experience on forbidding terrain. The opening 800m climb on tiring scree is followed by a crumbly approach to a narrow pass, snowbound well into summer. A plunging, dizzy descent to a refuge is followed by a straightforward path around the Pelmo's southern base.

Here a short detour leads to the *orme*, Italian for 'footprints', namely fossilised dinosaur tracks on a huge slab exposed by a fortuitous rockfall. Dating back 220 million years to when the Dolomites resembled the Caribbean, 100 footprints have been linked to three dinosaurs two metres tall, who apparently enjoyed splashing around in the tropical shallows. As the tides receded, the prints filled up with deposits that gradually hardened. A shorter, Grade 2, 2hr 30min return walk is feasible to admire the site.

THE PELMO

Awe-inspiring from any angle, the Pelmo towers over the Boite and Zoldo valleys, its giant throne-like appearance and horizontal rock layering easily recognisable from afar. Its exposed ledges and dizzy steep-sided flanks were explored over the ages by local chamois hunters long before the peak was officially claimed by British pioneer John Ball in 1857.

The mountain was described by Gilbert and Churchill in 1864: 'For an hour the Pelmo … rose clear above the near green slopes of the valley northward … all but the very battlements free from cloud; a pale salmon-tinted, glistening mass, shooting upward from its hidden base below into the eddying mists above; a spectacle not of the earth but of the sky, in its cerulean tints and aerial architecture.'

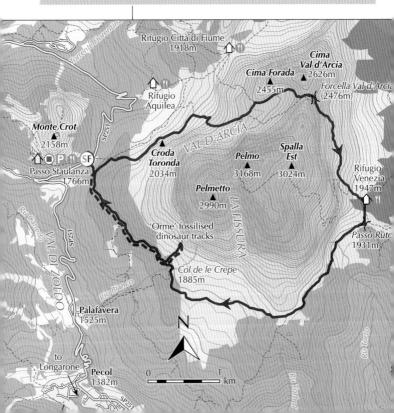

Short route: the Orme (2hr 30min return)

Leave Passo Staulanza on n.472 in the direction of Rifugio Venezia in gentle ascent in woodland. Heading S, you cross marshy zones with the help of plank walkways. Around 2km on is a signpost pointing L for the Orme. The steep narrow path clambers up a stream, slippery going at times. Multi-coloured earth layers precede your arrival at the surprising slab studded with **fossilised dinosaur tracks** (2050m). Return the same way to Passo Staulanza.

Main route

Leave Passo Staulanza (1766m) on path n.472, in common with the Orme route. However, a matter of minutes uphill, fork L to head NE. Amid bountiful wild orchids, the path climbs through light wood past waterworks, to an easily missed fork: leave the path for Rifugio Città di Fiume and turn R on n.480 signed for Forada. A narrow path, it ascends NE, with a slight drop below Croda Toronda.

As you approach the massive walls of the Pelmo, the trees give way to immense tongues of scree in awesome Val d'Arcia (VdA), its blinding white rock colonised by thick mats of mountain avens and scented pinks. Proceed in constant ascent, following painted lettering for VdA. You ignore a branch L (a link with n.472) and then head up in wide curves to two prominent boulders with n.480 emblazoned on them, the going getting steeper and rougher.

The clear red-marked route ▶ bears diagonally L, a strenuous slog; one step forward, two steps back in places due to the mobile scree. You finally gain the grassy shoulder below Cima Forada, and join the path from Forcella Forada. Keep R on the Sentiero Flaibani, carefully following red paint splashes through a jungle of tumbled rocks, where walkers are dwarfed. Surprisingly, bright clumps of Rhaetian poppies flourish in this wilderness. After hugging the rock face at the base of Cima Val d'Arcia you cross this immense valley and ascend very steeply, finally gaining **Forcella Val d'Arcia** (2476m, **2hr 30min**). ▶

Don't be tempted by the faint path that cuts up R to a ridge below the Pelmo's shrinking glacier, as it is dangerous and subject to rockfalls.

The haunt of perpetually hungry alpine choughs, this dizzy perch gives views over the forested Boite valley, dominated by the Antelao pyramid and the wild Marmarole.

The descent path disappears over the edge as a dramatic plunge, but take heart – the rubble is soft and, once you dig your heels in, makes for a relatively straightforward descent. Heading ESE, it reaches a rock face and is guided by a series of fixed cables for narrow passages on crumbly terrain. After a minor saddle, n.472 veers S and soon becomes much easier as the hut comes into sight, albeit still a long way below. Down flowered slopes of thrift you skirt the base of the prominent east shoulder (Spalla Est) prior to **Rifugio Venezia** (1947m, **1hr**). ◀

The magnificent return leg hugs the base of the Pelmo, staying close to its soaring flanks. Head over S to **Passo Rutorto** (1931m), then take n.472 downhill SW via slippery clay banks to a stream bed, close to a marshy basin once frequented by prehistoric hunters. The ensuing climb through wood and alpenrose leads to

It is beautifully placed for views and the home-made soups and cakes aren't bad either. Constructed in 1892, this was the very first Italian Alpine Club refuge in the Dolomites.

The Pelmo and its cleft clearly seen from the path

open muddy pasture, with marvellous views over to the Civetta, and soon even to the snowbound Marmolada. In a westerly direction, you traverse a veritable sea of dwarf pine, but it is low enough not to obstruct the progressively modified vistas to the Pelmo itself, including the marvellous cleft La Fissura which separates the Pelmetto (little Pelmo) from the main body.

Soon after **Col de le Crepe** (1885m), n.472 comes to the **'Orme' turn-off** (1890m, **1hr 30min**). Here a narrow path R clambers up a minor stream where the going can be slippery. Next are layers of multi-coloured earth before you reach the huge slab studded with **fossilised dinosaur tracks** (2050m). Allow an extra 30min for this recommended detour.

Back at the turn-off, turn R for the last leg which consists of a series of pleasant ups and downs through pretty larch wood, with hosts of wine-red martagon lilies and purple orchids. You finally emerge on the grassy realms of **Passo Staulanza** (**1hr**).

WALK 20
Gores de Federa

Start/Finish	Campo di Sotto, Cortina
Distance	15km
Ascent/Descent	770m
Grade	2
Walking time	4hr (2hr 30min if jeep service is used for return to Campo di Sotto)
Map	Tabacco n.03 scale 1:25,000
Refreshments	Lago di Pianozes, Malga Federa
Access	A local Cortina bus runs to Campo di Sotto. By car either park here or drive the half kilometre up to Lago di Pianozes. Needs-be at walk's end, a jeep taxi service (tel 346 0825609) is on hand to ferry weary walkers from Malga Federa to Campo di Sotto.

On the outskirts of Cortina, this exciting walk follows a cascading stream through marvellous ravines and canyons, to emerge at a beautifully placed farm-cum-café with vast views over the Boite basin and its mountains. The name Gores de Federa means 'canyons of the Federa', the main stream.

From Campo di Sotto (1127m) walk S up the narrow road labelled n.432. Ignore the turnoff for **Lago di Pianozes** (car park, café-restaurant) and continue uphill, pacing yourself on the steep gradient. At the signed fork **Col Purin** (1350m) turn L onto the start of the Gores de Federa (GdF) route. Soft underfoot, the path climbs easily through woodland. At a lane it divides: a short *sentiero attrezzato* (aided) variant goes L to follow a stream with cable stretches along its rock walls – a sure foot and low water levels are essential; whereas the normal route goes

A modern bridge crosses the Rio Federa

120

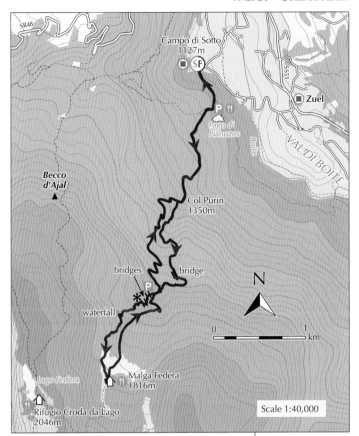

R to a lookout. The two rejoin soon afterwards and cross the stream on a marvellous modern **bridge**.

You continue up through woodland to join the road near a **car park**. Here the GdF route turns R off the tarmac to zigzag up and cross two more bridges over an awesome ravine where the torrent cascades. After a tiny **lookout** squeezed between overhangs you follow rock corridors before dropping to the stream bed on an iron walkway.

121

Wonderful views to the Sorapiss and over the magnificent Cortina basin.

Steps lead back out to woodland and on to a picnic table near a marvellous **waterfall**. A little more ascent sees you cross pastureland to reach superbly located farm-cum-eatery-cum-accommodation **Malga Federa** (1816m, **2hr 30min**). ◀

Return to **Campo di Sotto** by following the narrow surfaced road. Allow **1hr 30min**. Or be lazy and take the jeep taxi back.

WALK 21
Around the Croda da Lago

Start/Finish	Ponte di Rocurto
Distance	13.5km
Ascent/Descent	950m
Grade	2+
Walking time	5hr
Map	Tabacco n.03 scale 1:25,000
Refreshments	Rifugio Palmieri
Access	A summer Dolomiti Bus from Cortina via Pocol runs to Passo Giau. Ask the driver to let you off near Ponte di Rocurto, 4km from Pocol. Car owners can park along the road.

A short distance southwest of Cortina, the Croda da Lago is a relatively modest Dolomite formation, but memorable for its elegant slender profile and ridge of jagged points reminiscent of a recumbent dinosaur. This lovely walk circles the mountain and takes in the unusual neighbouring Lastoni di Formin – a gigantic, inclined table-like slab that rears up alongside. It is composed of Dürrenstein dolomite, boasting a record thickness of 450 metres here.

Overall, this walk rates slightly above average in terms of difficulty, with height gain and loss making it a fair hike not to mention a steep knee-challenging descent, but all effort is amply compensated by wonderful views. You visit the lovely alpine hut Rifugio Palmieri, set on the shore of pretty Lago Federa. The following section sees few walkers as it traverses rugged rock-ridden terrain.

The path from Ponte di Rocurto

Close to the bridge known as Ponte di Rocurto (1700m), a signpost points you E onto path n.437. After a dip across a stream you enter lovely shady woods then, not far along, traverse the Rio Costeana via a photogenic log bridge. It's a pretty route through sweet-smelling conifer wood thick with bilberries. After a zigzag ascent you pass high over a gorge. On the other side a short climb concludes at a marked junction close to **Cason di Formin** (1845m, **30min**), a log cabin. Ignore the fork R for Val di Formin (the return route) and proceed E on n.434. A steepish stretch follows, after which reward comes in the shape of a marvellous **lookout point**. ▶

From here you follow the Val Negra and it is easy, mostly level walking to pretty Lago Federa and then on to charming **Rifugio Palmieri** (2046m, **1hr**) aka Croda da Lago, located beneath the graceful eastern wall of the eponymous mountain. ▶

A marvellous, straightforward route (n.434) leads S below soaring rock points up to **Forcella Ambrizola**

The breadth of the view is quite astonishing after all the trees: clockwise are the isolated Cinque Torri, the pointed Nuvolau, the Tofane, Pomagagnon over Cortina and the magnificent Sorapiss.

The hut was named for a WW2 partisan from Bologna.

123

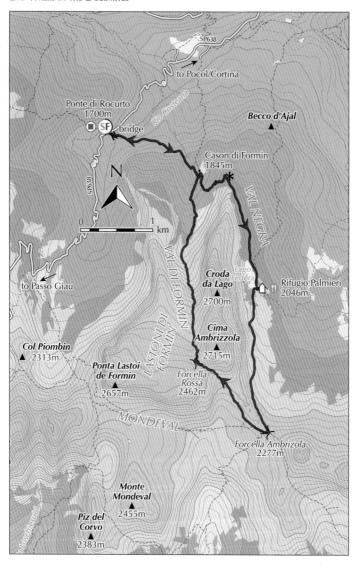

to Pocol/Cortina

Ponte di Rocurto
1700m

SF bridge

Becco d'Ajal ▲

Cason di Formin
1845m

N

VAL NEGRA

SP638

0   1
━━━━━━━━
km

VAL DI FORMIN

*Croda
da Lago*
▲
2700m

Lago
Federa

Rifugio Palmieri
2046m

to Passo Giau

LASTONI DI
FORMIN

*Cima
Ambrizzola*
▲
2715m

Col Piombin
▲ 2313m

*Ponta Lastoi
de Formin*
▲
2657m

*Forcella
Rossa*
2462m

MONDEVAL

Forcella Ambrizola
2277m

*Monte
Mondeval*
▲
2455m

*Piz del
Corvo*
▲
2383m

(2277m, **45min**), close to the Becco di Mezzodì. This pass spells entry to the broad swathe of the Mondeval basin, which slopes southwards dotted with grazing sheep – oblivious to the majesty around them.

THE MONDEVAL PASTURE BASIN

Around 10,000 years ago Mesolithic hunters would trap ibex and deer here by blocking off its accesses. An enormous quantity of implements in bone, flint and rock crystal has been unearthed close to an overhanging boulder-cum-shelter, not to mention the skeleton of a 40-year-old Cro-Magnon male in a ritualised burial. The intriguing finds are on display at the Selva di Cadore museum in Val Fiorentina (www.museoselvadicadore.it).

Turn R (NW) on n.436 towards Passo Giau, but fork off R after 5min for the steady climb on n.435 to the breathtaking **Forcella Rossa** (2462m, **45min**), aka Formin, directly under Cima Ambrizzola. ▸ Bearing N, the path follows the west wall of the Croda da Lago down Val di Formin. Waymarks are few and faded, so keep your eyes skinned. The descent sees you heading quite steeply at times navigating scree and rock outcrops. The valley

The Lastoni di Formin (great slabs) extend westward in this bizarre landscape, rent with gigantic cracks that run deep into the rock.

Snow lies late on the Lastoni di Formin slabs

narrows and you clamber over boulders in the company of a cascading stream criss-crossed several times – watch your step on slippery rocks. Larch trees and grass are finally reached, a welcome return to greenery. Then you're at the junction near **Cason di Formin** (1845m, **1hr 30min**). Turn L onto n.437 for the final leg back to the road at **Ponte di Rocurto** (**30min**).

WALK 22
The Cinque Torri

Start/Finish	Bai de Dones chairlift
Distance	7.5km
Ascent/Descent	400m
Grade	2
Walking time	3hr 30min
Map	Tabacco n.03 scale 1:25,000
Refreshments	Bai de Dones, Rifugio Scoiattoli
Access	Cortina Express and Dolomiti Bus services from Cortina to Passo Falzarego stop at Bai de Dones in summer. There is an ample car park.

This beautiful circuit leads around the Cinque Torri, a clump of unusual jagged rock towers and a magnet for acrobatic climbers. Despite the name – 'five towers' – there are actually 11 in all, if you count the minor columns, although the Torre Trephor was irredeemably lost when it collapsed in a heap in 2004, thankfully without injuring anyone.

The walk also explores a convoluted network of trenches and positions from the years of World War 1, an open-air museum that serves as a poignant reminder of the folly of war. You will undoubtedly be tempted to follow more of the signposted routes, so allow extra time. Clear paths are followed all the way and there are constantly fantastic views scanning the Cortina basin.

The fascinating area is justifiably popular, visitor numbers augmented by the *seggiovia* (chairlift), which can be used on the outward stretch if desired. However once the trenches are left behind, walkers are thin on the ground. By all means link this route with Walk 23, which climbs to the superb Nuvolau.

From the car park and chairlift at Bai de Dones (1889m), turn uphill to head W on path n.424. Through lovely

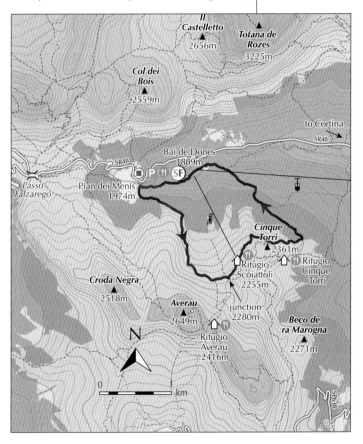

127

Possible link to
Walk 23 here.

The name of this
welcoming family-
run refuge refers to
the famous Cortina-
based rock climbing
team, the Squirrels.

*The walk drops in
on a cavern under
the Torre Inglese*

woodland filled with streams and marshland, and vivid
with wild orchids and cotton grass, you climb easily to
Pian dei Menis (1974m, **20min**). ◄ Here, branch L on
n.440, a delightfully graded path SE. Through light wood,
it gains height and emerges on open mountainside and
a ski slope. At a **junction** (2280m), it traverses NE on a
broad track that descends to the magnificent belvedere
Rifugio Scoiattoli (2255m, **1hr**). ◄ The giant Tofane and
the Lagazuoi stand out over the valley, while close at
hand the Cinque Torri teeth emerge from grassy gums.
Behind you, the twins of Monte Averau and Nuvolau rear
up abruptly.

At the chairlift, turn L (N) downhill, on the path
heading into the reconstructed trench system. You soon
encounter a series of points of interest marked by letters.
At point A branch L for a rest area with soldier figures in
uniform. Return to the main path and go L past observation positions to C, then take the short detour to a lookout. Resume the main path and you soon bear R to point

E, a roofed artillery position, immediately after which you descend steep timber steps with a rope handrail, to an excavated section.

At the bottom go sharp R then L along a protected passageway with brilliant views across the valley, concluding at panoramic point M. Now begins the little-trodden part of this walk, clearly marked in red and white stripes. You veer R through a rock gateway that leads close to the north faces of the **Cinque Torri** – a jagged, broken, crazy jungle of rock towers.

A narrower path drops to a cavern below the soaring Torre Inglese, before it picks its way through the smashed rock left by the collapsed Torre Trephor. A little further on, at a signed fork, keep L on n.425 (unless you wish to detour to Rifugio Cinque Torri). This soon enters a long series of trenches, which wind gradually down E, with brilliant alternating outlooks over the Cortina basin. As the path reaches a minor surfaced road closed to private traffic (**1hr 30min**), fork L to the next bend, where the signed path resumes NW through the wood. This lovely stretch is shaded by tall conifers and brightened by alpenrose. It's a gentle descent past a tiny lake to head back to **Bai de Dones** (**40min**).

WALK 23
Up the Nuvolau

Start/Finish	Rifugio Col Gallina, near Passo Falzarego
Distance	9.6km
Ascent/Descent	700m
Grade	2
Walking time	4hr 10min
Map	Tabacco n.03 scale 1:25,000
Refreshments	Rifugio Col Gallina, Rifugio Averau, Rifugio Nuvolau
Access	In summer Dolomiti Bus and Cortina Express services on the Cortina-Passo Falzarego run stop near Rifugio Col Gallina. There is roadside parking.

This stunning circuit skirts the Averau while it heads for its final destination, the Nuvolau, one of the best known – and easiest to reach – Dolomite mountains in the beautiful Cortina basin. Breathtaking 360-degree views are the reward for a little uphill effort. There are clear paths to follow, masses of wildflowers to admire and hospitable refuges for a relaxing lunch or refreshments. What more could anyone ask from an alpine walk?

The central part of this walk is well-trodden due to the chairlift from Bai de Dones, which can be used to shorten either the outward or return leg, followed by a bus back to the start.

From the road near Rifugio Col Gallina (2054m), signposts point under a short, winter chairlift for path n.419. This begins climbing steadily S through conifer wood. You pass rock caverns dating back to the WW1 years en route to **Lago Limedes** (2171m). ◄ The path meanders through thinning trees and across brightly flowered grass-rock inclines, following the base of elongated Croda Negra. You gain height little by little on ever-rockier terrain to **Forcella Averau** (2435m), the stronghold of a flock of jet-black alpine choughs, where the path merges with n.441 from Passo Falzarego.

The shallow water reflects the sheer block of the Averau, which rises nearby.

Turn L heading SE for mostly level – if narrow – walking cutting across scree and skirting the crumbling southern wall of Monte Averau. It concludes at **Rifugio Averau** (2416m, **1hr 40min**). ◄

This cheery refuge boasts excellent food and a great terrace looking to the Marmolada and much more.

There is a signed path uphill of the building that climbs to the long ridge R (SE) up the Nuvolau. The straightforward and popular path n.439 follows this unusual broad rock incline for 150 metres to charming **Rifugio Nuvolau** (2575m), perched on the eponymous summit. Now the property of the Alpine Club of Cortina, the original building dated back to the late 1800s and could be reached on horseback via a special bridle track. ◄ The atmosphere here is unique, and on those days when the mountain does not live up to its name – *nuvola* means cloud – the views are breathtaking, ranging as far away as the snow-capped Ortler.

Austrian artillery destroyed the hut during WW1 so the present building dates back to 1930 (extensive modernisation was carried out in 2021).

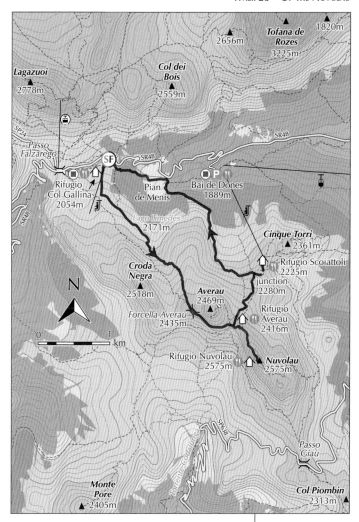

Well rewarded, return to **Rifugio Averau** (2416m,
1hr) then turn R (NNE). A wide track descends over

Rifugio Averau nestles at the foot of the Averau

the ski slopes to a **junction** (2280m) signed for Pian dei Menis.

Alternative route via Rifugio Scoiattoli and the chairlift
By all means continue to nearby **Rifugio Scoiattoli** (2225m) and the strange Cinque Torri rock formations. The maze of trenches and shelters alongside date back to World War 1 – they have been restored for visitors and are explored in Walk 22. The chairlift can also be used for the descent to **Bai de Dones** (1889m), which is close to the road with a bus stop 3.5km below Passo Falzarego.

Main route
Branch L (NW) on n.440 to traverse a rocky mountain-side. With amazing views to the Tofane, the delightful path narrows, crossing sparse wood with mixed conifers and dwarf pines on the final stretch. Amid a colourful array of wild flowers, it reaches the marshy meadows of **Pian dei Menis** (1974m, **1hr 10min**). Now fork L on path n.424, sticking to the left-hand side of the nearby road, to go back to **Rifugio Col Gallina** (**20min**).

WALK 24

Skirting the Tofana di Rozes

Start/Finish	Da Strobel car park, near Passo Falzarego
Distance	13km
Ascent/Descent	800m
Grade	2
Walking time	4hr 45min
Map	Tabacco n.03 scale 1:25,000
Refreshments	Da Strobel, Rifugio Dibona
Access	Summer Dolomiti Bus and Cortina Express services on the Cortina-Passo Falzarego run stop near Da Strobel restaurant opposite Rifugio Col Gallina. There is roadside parking.

This thrilling route follows a path that coasts high above the road maintaining 2300m altitude at the foot of the amazing Tofana di Rozes, a spectacular Dolomite mountain with a sheer southern face that soars to a dizzy 3225m. The outlook is simply breathtaking every way you look, including over the splendid valley basin where the renowned resort of Cortina nestles. En route, constructions dating back to the years of World War 1 are encountered. Good clear paths are followed, with a narrowish central section on scree.

A little over halfway, Rifugio Dibona makes a good place for lunch for walkers not equipped with a picnic.

From Da Strobel restaurant and car park (2024m), a well-worn path signed for the *Via Ferrata degli Alpini* climbs easily through dwarf pines, where you will be in the company of climbers laden with gear. Up at a path junction, fork R (E) on n.423. This is an old military road that cuts below Col dei Bos, past dazzling cliffs where edelweiss and devil's claw grow in crannies. A derelict **wartime hospital** (2166m), which dates back to 1917, stands just round the corner in a sheltered cleft under the Torri del Falzarego. Here, you part ways with the via ferrata buffs.

Wartime hospital dating back to 1917

Leaving the clearing, the wide track heads gently downhill to the **R'Agaroles** intersection (2035m, **45min**). In the likely company of chamois, fork L on n.412 up to a short tunnel. Perfectly graded broad curves lead

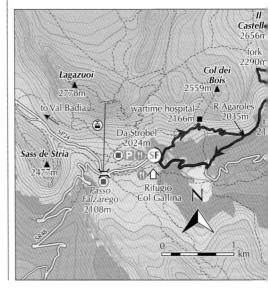

uphill NE, although several short cuts are feasible. Near the minor Rozes outcrop, ignore a 2183m fork for the moment (the return route slots back in here). The way soon narrows to a path NNW, accompanied by WW1 trenches in the shadow of the towering Castelletto outcrop. ▸

The side of this formation was blown to smithereens by explosives during the war.

Turn R (E) at the **fork** (2290m, **1hr**) for n.404, in common with the Alta Via 1 trek. In constant ascent towards the awesome rock corner, it has ever-improving views over the Cortina basin. Ignore branches up L for

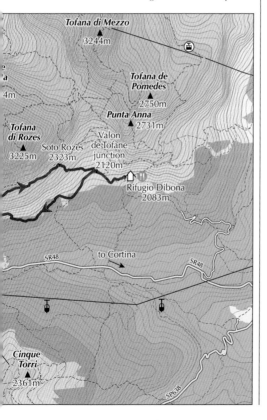

135

the Gallerie del Castelletto (unless you're equipped with headlamp and via ferrata kit), and continue across multi-coloured earth layers as the way narrows, feeling a little exposed at times.

Further around, at the **Soto Rozes junction** (2323m) you fork R downhill on the edge of an immense eroded gully, where rock needles seem to grow out of the scree. Down amid bushy vegetation once again, you pass the cableway loading point for Rifugio Giussani, near the **Valon de Tofane** junction (2120m, **1hr**). The return route forks off here but it's a pity to miss the friendly hut ahead. ◄

If you wish, the hut can be detoured to save half an hour.

Rifugio Dibona (2083m) stands **15min** SE down the jeep track, should you feel the urge to enjoy a delicious cooked lunch.

Afterwards, return to the **Valon de Tofane** junction and head W on n.412. This is a narrow but clear path that traverses the immense mountainside about 300m below the outward route. It is level for the most part, but climbs a little towards the end to cross a minor rockfall and rejoin the military road followed earlier at the **fork** (2183m, **1hr**).

Turn L downhill and go through the tunnel to the **R'Agaroles** intersection (**15min**). Here, instead of retracing your steps uphill via the derelict hospital, turn L on n.412 in gentle descent to the roadside and the old Magistrato alle Acque building. Go R on the unmarked track parallel to the tarmac, cutting the bends, to soon arrive back at **Da Strobel car park** (2024m, **30min**).

Rifugio Dibona

WALK 25

The Lagazuoi Tunnels

Start/Finish	Passo Falzarego
Distance	6km (+1.5km for extension)
Ascent/Descent	600m (+30m for extension)
Grade	3
Walking time	3hr 15min (+30min for extension)
Maps	Tabacco n.03 or n.07 scale 1:25,000
Refreshments	Passo Falzarego, Rifugio Lagazuoi
Access	In summer Dolomiti Bus and Cortina Express from Cortina reach the pass, as do SAD buses from Val Badia. You can take the Lagazuoi cable car for the ascent, and cut 1hr 45min off the walk time.

The strategic pass where the walk starts is close to the former Italian–Austrian border and saw tragic events sweep through with the outbreak of World War 1. Needless to say, there was devastating loss of life on both sides. The surrounding mountains still bear extensive evidence including a total of 11 incredible near-vertical tunnels bored through rock. One, dating from June 1917, has been restored with steps, ladders and cables, enabling walkers to experience an 1100 metre-long *galleria* (tunnel) that climbs 230m with a 45-degree gradient inside the mountain. From their stronghold on the Cengia Martini ledge, the Italians intended to dislodge the Austrians on the Lagazuoi Piccolo summit. The mountain face was radically altered by explosions – the enormous cone of detritus directly under the cable car is proof.

After an uphill path (or cable-car ride) from the pass, you follow the tunnel in descent. It is exhilarating but recommended for experienced walkers only, as it is steep, slippery and has a long section with no natural light. A headlamp is essential and leaves your hands free to grip the cable, while gloves will keep them warm.

Passo Falzarego has café-restaurants, tantalising alpine kitsch, a good selection of maps and an info kiosk alongside the cable car where head torches, helmets and all manner of gear can be hired.

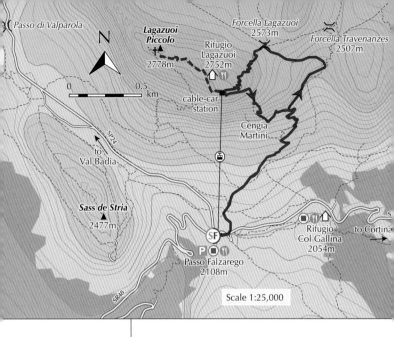

Tucked up under the soaring Punta Berrino on your left are old huts and fortifications; the slopes are scattered with timber and barbed wire.

This magnificent viewpoint overlooks the vast, gentle, stony slopes of the Alpe di Lagazuoi, backed by the sheer flanks of the Punte di Fanes and Cima del Lago.

At Passo Falzarego (2108m) you need path n.402. It strikes out NE, alongside winter ski slopes, to embark on the 650m ascent. Somewhat monotonous scree terrain can be expected with innumerable steep zigzags, but this is amply compensated by wide-reaching views. Half an hour up, it ignores the fork L for the strategic ledge Cengia Martini and tunnels (the descent route), with plenty of rock windows visible. ◀

Keep L at the fork for Forcella Lagazuoi to ascend a steep ski slope that passes above Forcella Travenanzes. You flank the elongated rock barrier of Lagazuoi Grande to gain **Forcella Lagazuoi** (2573m, **1hr 15min**). ◀

Now the path SW follows the Muraglia Rocciosa crest, pitted with Austrian tunnels and helpful information boards. A clear path then zigzags up to the **cable-car station** (**30min**). A few steep metres away is **Rifugio Lagazuoi** (2752m), which boasts a top-class restaurant as well as a marvellous panoramic terrace, and name plates to help you identify the multitude of mountains.

Extension to Lagazuoi Piccolo (30min return)

From the terrace at the side of the building proceed onto a metal walkway attached to the rock face before joining a broad path up to the cross and breathtaking lookout that is the summit of **Lagazuoi Piccolo** (2778m). After taking in the spectacular views, return to Rifugio Lagazuoi.

The cable car up to the Lagazuoi passes above wartime debris

Main route

From the cable-car station, follow the arrows for the *galleria*, just below the concrete platform. A clear path with a cable handrail makes its way round to the L (E), past fortifications and via a crest where trench walkways have been reconstructed. The path enters a doorway and 'disappears' into a hole (**10min**) for the start of the tunnel – a glance inside gives an idea of what's to come. A series of 'windows' provides dizzying views and the guiding cable is continuous, as is a series of steps, although the constant presence of water makes it slippery going – the difficulty is compounded by a lack of natural light at times. ▶

There are storage depots, cramped sleeping quarters and eerie side tunnels en route.

After about an hour of heading down, you return to daylight on a broad ledge adjoining the Cengia Martini. The route proceeds L via a snow-choked gully and a final short tunnel. From here it's a steep scramble and zigzag to join path n.402 for the final drop to **Passo Falzarego** (**1hr 20min**).

PASSO FALZAREGO

Passo Falzarego – from *falso re* or 'false king' – is linked with legend. This was once the realm of the Fanes people, whose greedy king betrayed his subjects in return for riches. But his karma caught up with him and he turned into rock – his petrified profile stands out to this day on the Lagazuoi Piccolo mountain – his long beard and crown of rocky points clearly visible from below.

WALK 26

The Kaiserjäger Route

Start/Finish	Passo di Valparola
Distance	9.5km
Ascent/Descent	700m
Grade	2–3
Walking time	4hr
Maps	Tabacco n.03 or n.07 scale 1:25,000
Refreshments	Rifugio Valparola, Rifugio Lagazuoi
Access	In summer SAD and Cortina Express buses on the Val Badia-Cortina run stop at Passo di Valparola.

This is a quite brilliant and extremely rewarding circuit on the Lagazuoi, just round the corner from the more popular area accessible by cable car. The outward ascent follows a supply route constructed up a sheltered gully by Austrian Kaiserjäger troops in World War 1. It has been restored with timber reinforcements, iron rungs and cable and even a short suspension bridge, and nowadays can be appreciated by walkers who don't have a problem with narrow paths and exposure. After the breathtaking summit of Lagazuoi Piccolo followed by the nearby refuge, you proceed across a limestone plateau where very few people venture, before looping back down to the pass where it all began. All in all, this is a superb (although not simple) day's outing. Rifugio Valparola, at the walk start, offers great meals and guest rooms with a view, as does Rifugio Lagazuoi higher up.

TRE SASSI FORT

It's well worth visiting the museum set up in the Tre Sassi fort (www.cortinamuseoguerra.it) near the walk start. It stands in the shadow of sloping Sasso di Stria, riddled with wartime paths and passageways that invite further exploration.

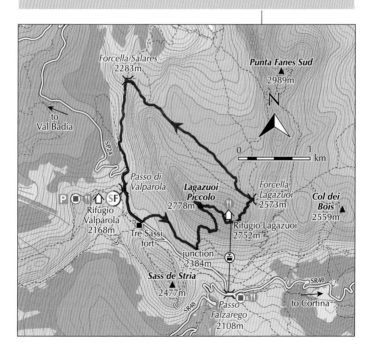

From Passo di Valparola (2168m), walk along the road to the old **fort** and museum. Directly opposite, a path strikes out E in gentle steady ascent. Leading across rockscape below the momentous wall of the Lagazuoi, it touches on a small fort and a climbing wall, before a **junction** (2384m, **30min**), where a path from Passo Falzarego joins up. (Should you have inadvertently ended up on a lower variant, continue along trenches to a prominent boulder then fork L up to the 2384m junction.) Much steeper now, the path zigzags up the scree, approaching the rock face where iron staples lead up a gully.

Next comes an exposed aided ledge and a suspension bridge across an awesome cleft. The aided path climbs to an outcrop once hosting troop quarters and dormitories. Not far up is a fork where you keep L (NW) for a drawn-out dizzy and narrow stretch, accompanied by cable in places. **Take this slowly and watch your**

Walkers on the Kaiserjäger route, high above Passo Falzarego

step. It finally concludes at a modest saddle on the crest, where you turn R to the cross on the spectacular top of **Lagazuoi Piccolo** (2778m, **1hr 15min**). ▶

Continue ESE along the well-trodden broad crest to a metal walkway that leads onto the fabulous panoramic terrace of **Rifugio Lagazuoi** (2752m, **15min**).

The departure station for the cable car to Passo Falzarego and the start of the WW1 tunnels (see Walk 25) are not far below. From there keep L down the vast incline alongside the Muraglia Rocciosa, punctuated with tunnels and living quarters with illustrated panels. Further downhill, you reach the saddle of **Forcella Lagazuoi** (2573m, **20min**) at the base of bright red earth-rock layers and avalanche barriers with an inspiring angle to the Tofane. Fork sharp L on n.20 then L again on n.20a, a lovely path across undulating plateau enjoying the superb Cima del Lago and Cima Scotoni. In the realms of the Parco Naturale Fanes-Sennes-Braies follow red/white waymarks carefully as you descend gradually to a short narrow stretch preceding grassy **Forcella Salares** (2283m, **1hr**), where edelweiss bloom. ▶

Turn L (S) here for the precipitous gully, easily negotiated thanks to reinforced timber zigzags. At the bottom the path begins a lovely coast through light wood of Arolla and larch. Rivers of scree have invaded the path in spots. An old track leads L up to the road where it's a short stroll up to **Passo di Valparola** (**40min**). ▶

The fantastic views range to the Tofane, Pelmo, Civetta, Marmolada and Sella massif among many, many others.

The outlook here takes in the marvellous spread-out Puez-Odle and Sella groups, as well as Rifugio Valparola on the road below.

The broad saddle between the Falzarego and Valparola passes is strewn with a chaos of massive broken rocks and boulders, left by a long-melted glacier.

WALK 27
Round the Settsass

Start/Finish	Passo di Valparola
Distance	13km (11km without Setsas summit)
Ascent/Descent	950m (650m without Setsas summit)
Grade	2
Walking time	5hr 30min (4hr without Setsas summit)
Map	Tabacco n.07 scale 1:25,000
Refreshments	Rifugio Valparola
Access	In summer SAD and Cortina Express buses on the Val Badia-Cortina run stop at Passo di Valparola.

Dwarfed into relative insignificance by the outstanding Dolomite massifs of Lagazuoi and Cunturines in its proximity, the Settsass (seven stones) stands isolated; a jagged ridge rising out of gently rolling pasture. Reaching a maximum height of 2571m above sea level from a base that clocks in at 2100m, it stretches in a west–east curve for 3km overall. The northern aspect is a vast, gentle incline, while the southern side declines quite abruptly in a series of magnificent walls and sheer towers. It boasts an easily reachable summit that rates as hugely panoramic. You'll make good use of the PeakFinder app today!

This magnificent circuit walk also guarantees brilliant spreads of wildflowers, as well as marmots and even chamois. Waymarking is abundant and other walkers few and far between. There is a non-stop 300m ascent to reach the actual summit (avoidable with a saving of 1hr 30min), but the rest of the route can hardly be described as level either, the innumerable ups and downs making for tiring going. You pass no refreshment points and the only shelter is the Bivacco Sief hut, so be prepared for a full day out.

From the signposts behind the refuge building at Passo di Valparola (2168m), take path n.24 and the Giro del Settsass (the Settsass Circuit). Swinging L, the path skirts the knoll sheltering the building, coasts above the lake and dips to a junction signed for Pralongià, where you turn R on n.24.

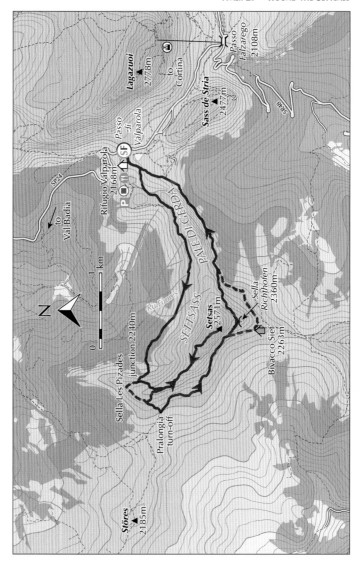

A gradual climb W across red clay slopes leads to a broad saddle where you head SW along the mountain's northern flank. You pass a huddle of military ruins on slopes dotted with crosses fashioned with old timbers. Several hands-on clambers with a little exposure are encountered as the path continues essentially W beneath Monte Castello, the ground continually rising and falling.

Marsh marigolds on the lake near Passo Valparola

You cross the grassy basin of Val Pudres, where your approach will undoubtedly be signalled by the alarm whistles of the marmot colony's sentinels. At a **junction** (2240m, **1hr 30min**), turn L for 'Cime Setsas', leaving n.24 for the time being. ▸

Red and white waymarking leads diagonally SW up a grass-rock flank, carpeted with purple oxytropis, to gain a red earth crest (2340m) and extraordinary views over the lush pastures of Pralongià to the Marmolada as well as the Sella massif. Marked by cairns, the path proceeds SE, sticking to the sloping northwestern side of the main ridge up a massive rock slab. You finally emerge at breathtaking **Setsas** (2571m, **45min**) and its wooden cross on the plunging edge. ▸

From the peak, return the same way to the red earth crest (2340m) and, instead of taking the outward route, keep L and follow the waymarks easily down to rejoin path n.24. The **Pralongià turn-off** (2200m, **45min**) is not far on.

Now it's SE on n.23, past picturesque old timber huts and onto rocky terrain beneath the Montagna della Corte. A gradual ascent leads to several quite narrow crumbly passages, where a sure step is essential.

About 45min on, below an evident col, search for the faint path forking up L – it starts in the vicinity of faded lettering for 'Pralongià' painted on a rock.

Alternative via Bivacco Sief

Instead of climbing to Sella Richthofen, this more straightforward route sticks to the lower path, n.23. It gains a clay-grass saddle with the wooden hut **Bivacco Sief** (2263m, **20min**) and a crucifix. The path soon bears up L (NE) to join the Sella Richthofen main route.

Main route

It quickly reaches **Sella Richthofen** (2360m, **1hr**), aka Forcella del Settsass. ▸

The walk proceeds on a decent path E, which is soon joined by n.23, before it drops gradually and almost imperceptibly along the marvellous southern flanks of

To avoid the summit climb, stay on n.24 for the *Sella Les Pizades* and pick up the main route at the junction just around the corner.

The 360-degree views include the Richthofen Riff, with its fossil beds, directly below.

A short detour leads to a WW1 observatory that looks over to Col di Lana.

The return path is dwarfed by the Pale di Gerda

the Settsass beneath the Pale di Gerda and the impressive Torre Gabriella and Torre Margherita.

◀ A brief climb followed by a rock gully with a guiding cable lead up N into a marshy pasture basin with fluffy cotton grass, not to mention wartime caverns and trenches that were part of the Austrian 'Edelweiss' positions and supply line. The road and Austrian fort come into sight, and the path quickly reaches the junction with n.24 before ambling back to **Passo di Valparola** (**1hr 30min**).

As well as profusions of edelweiss on the open terrain, martagon lilies shelter among the Arolla and dwarf mountain pines.

SETTSASS

Settsass gained acclaim through the work of 19th-century German palaeontologists and geologists in search of the key to unravelling the mystery of the formation of the Dolomites. The most noteworthy was Baron Ferdinand von Richthofen, whose ground-breaking 1860 treatise suggested their origin as a coral reef. On the mountain's southern side is the Richthofen Riff – a modest outcrop with exposed fossil-rich beds that proved fundamental to scholars.

WALK 28
Santa Croce Sanctuary

Start/Finish	Badia/Pedraces chair lift/bus stop
Distance	9.5km (7.5km using San Cassiano exit)
Ascent	100m
Descent	650m (450m using San Cassiano exit)
Grade	1–2
Walking time	3hr 15min (2hr 30min using San Cassiano exit)
Map	Tabacco n.07 scale 1:25,000
Refreshments	Pedraces, middle lift station, Ospizio Santa Croce, San Cassiano
Access	Pedraces in Val Badia has year-round SAD buses. Car parking near the lift.

This walk to the sanctuary of Santa Croce in Val Badia makes use of two summer lifts on the approach. Afterwards you descend through woods and hamlets with ancient shingle-roofed farmhouses and barns surrounded by manicured meadows. Characteristic of Val Badia, they were grouped together for protection in medieval times, forming self-sufficient units with their own collective oven and well.

A highly recommended alternative exit is given for San Cassiano, from where you can return to Pedraces by bus.

SASSO DELLA CROCE

In spring and autumn, processions of chanting villagers in traditional garb and bearing statues make pilgrimages to the evocative high-altitude mountain sanctuary of Santa Croce in Val Badia. The whitewashed church holds a miraculous painting of Christ as well as a relic of the cross. Alongside stands a timber-lined pilgrims' hospice, now an inviting refuge, dating from 1718, with accommodation and delicious meals at very reasonable prices. Towering dramatically above is marvellously elongated Sasso della Croce (Sas dla Crusc in Ladin), which Amelia Edwards in 1873 likened to 'a

Cathedral with two short spires' though from a different angle it resembles a crouching lion with massive haunches.

In times long gone a monstrous fire-breathing dragon terrorised Val Badia, demanding human victims. No shepherd or woodcutter dared venture out alone until the arrival of Gran Bracun aka Guglielmo Prack, a bold knight from Marebbe. Fresh from the Crusades in the Holy Land, he wasted no time in pursuing the dreaded monster to its lair at the foot of the sheer rock face of Sasso della Croce. Having slayed it, he left its bones to bleach in the sun.

> Its position, at the foot of precipitous cliffs beneath Sasso della Croce (which turns a glowing fleshy pink as it catches the afternoon sun), is simply perfect.

From the bus stop at Badia/Pedraces (1324m), it's a short stroll to the chairlift. It's a leisurely trip to the **middle station** (1840m) for a second leg on a modern gondola. From where you get off, a short path climbs to the extraordinarily photogenic church and sanctuary **Ospizio S Croce** (2045m, **30min**), or Ütia La Crusc in Ladin, or Heiligkreuz Hospiz in German. ◀ Directly across the valley is the spread-out Puez-Odle group.

Path n.15 moves off S into light wood and the realms of the Fanes-Sennes-Braies Nature Park, below

The church and refuge at Santa Croce

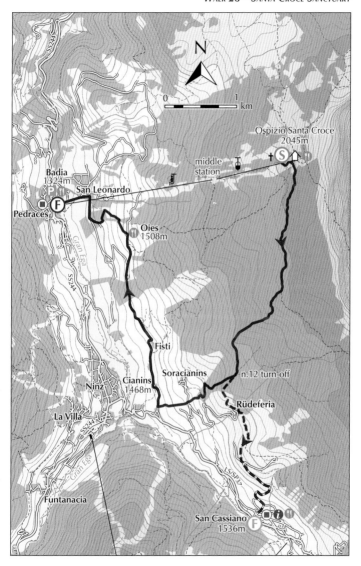

the mountain. Marked by stations of the cross, it coasts through springy masses of dwarf mountain pine which shelter roe deer, and there are several good lookout points over Val Badia and across to Sassongher. The broad path becomes a lane, dropping gradually. Ignore forks L for Forcella Medesc, but don't miss the clearly marked **n.12 turn-off** R (**1743m, 1hr 15min**).

Exit to San Cassiano (45min)

From the **n.12 turn-off**, keep S on n.15 out of the wood. You cross well-kept meadows to a huddle of farms (**Rüdeferia**) followed by an old timber mill on the banks of a stream, still complete with its waterwheel. After a series of modest ups and downs, a fenced-in stretch emerges on a narrow tarmac road. ◄ The road drops quickly towards the pedestrian town centre, along with cafés, the church and tourist office of **San Cassiano** (1536m). Further down at the main road you can take a bus back to Badia/Pedraces.

There are marvellous views of Piz dles Cunturines and the Cima Scotoni and Lagazuoi line-up.

Main route

Path n.12 follows a stream and drops steadily through wood, past one of many isolated rural hamlets. Down at a surfaced farm road, turn R along Tru dles Viles for the picturesque buildings of **Cianins** (1468m, **30min**). The narrow road leads N via a string of hamlets, each with interesting houses old and new, monumental barns and artistic crucifixes. This is a superbly scenic section high over Val Badia.

A little way after **Fisti**, you reach a wider road. Keep L for a brief section downhill, then take the next branch R, unsurfaced at first, for the brief climb to the sizeable settlement of **Oies** (1508m, **40min**), venerated as the birthplace of the 19th-century missionary PG Freinademetz. Just after panoramic coffee shop Tana dell'Orso, turn L (signed for Badia) on a lovely path lined with stations of the cross. Down at a minor road, go R towards the church and buildings of **San Leonardo**, then downhill back to the chairlift at **Badia/Pedraces** (**20min**).

WALK 29
Sass de Putia

Start/Finish	Passo delle Erbe
Distance	17.5km (14.5km without summit)
Ascent/Descent	1100m (600m without summit)
Grade	2–3
Walking time	6hr (4hr without summit)
Maps	Tabacco n.07 or n.030 scale 1:25,000
Refreshments	Passo delle Erbe, Sot Pùtia, Rifugio Genova, Ütia Vaciara, Ütia de Göma, Munt de Funella
Access	In summer SAD buses from Val Badia wend their way up to Passo delle Erbe, and a minibus comes up from Val di Funes.

Panoramic Passo delle Erbe/Würzjoch – the name a reference to grazing – is located at the very foot of Sass de Putia and makes for a perfect start point, with a hospitable guesthouse. The stunning circuit (*Rundweg*) described here takes in the peak. It is of intermediate difficulty, well within the range of the average walker. The sole exception is the summit ascent (Grade 3), as the final 150-metre leg is aided by a length of chain where it becomes steep and exposed. However, this is easily avoided by branching off to an easier and only slighter lower crest, as explained below. There are a number of farm huts turned cafés along the way, most with outdoor seating and farm-style menus. The term Ütia, commonly found here, is Ladin for 'summer farm'. A detour is also feasible via popular Rifugio Genova, although this adds half an hour to the walk time.

SASS DE PUTIA

Magnificent Sass de Putia/Sas de Pütia/Peitlerkofel is the most northerly of the Dolomites and the views from its 2875m peak are absolutely amazing. It is claimed that a grand total of 449 church spires in the Südtirol can be seen with a good pair of binoculars! This isolated mountain has contrasting aspects depending on the approach. From the south it is a gentle grass-covered slope, while from the north a series of jagged peaks top an abrupt 800m cliff, concluding with a seemingly impossible summit.

Geology buffs will find the environs fascinating, as the pale dolomite rock of Sass de Putia rises from dramatic multi-coloured strata where tiny fossilised shells are embedded.

Close at hand is the edge of a depression, where you can see the exposed dark red and grey strata underlying Sass de Putia.

Opposite the guesthouse at Passo delle Erbe (1978m), path n.8A/B strikes out S between two forestry tracks, past a modest eatery and through a wood of Arolla pines. ◄ Heather and bilberry shrubs line the way as you join a wide track past summer hay huts. Keep R at a **junction** (2067m) past the Sot Pütia hut to skirt the mountain on its southwestern side. The path narrows and alpenrose and mountain pine abound, while the views take in the impressive neighbouring Odle di Eores.

Lengthy crumbly tracts and reinforced pathways lead into a broad gully. Here you turn L joining path n.4 (Alta Via 2) for a relentless 200m climb, zigzagging between strewn boulders, a trickling stream and Rhaetian poppies. The final leg has timber traverses and steps, and more often than not is choked with snow in early summer. After all this barrenness, it comes as a genuine surprise to emerge at **Forcella di Putia** (2357m, **1hr 30min**) and be confronted with rich, rolling pastureland studded with yellow buttercups.

Alternative via Rifugio Genova

From **Forcella di Putia**, take path n.4 to head SW on a level. This will lead you through Passo di Poma to arrive at bustling, well-placed **Rifugio Genova** (2297m, **30min**), a great place for lunch. Afterwards, instead of retracing your steps, take the rough track n.35 NE in gentle descent to rejoin the main route at a **junction** (2140m, **20min**).

Main route

The path leading into the central fold of Sass de Putia goes sharp L (NE at first) into a shallow gully-valley

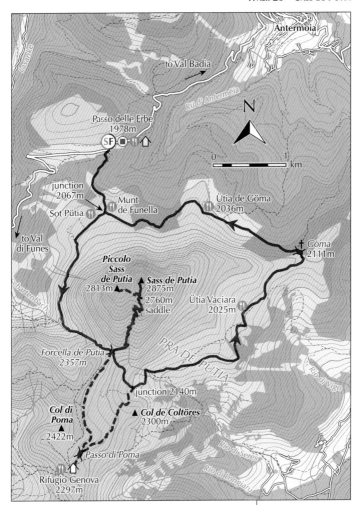

that often harbours late-lying snow. Wide curves climb
steadily – keep R at the fork around 2600m for a brief
rock crest passage and ever-improving views. At a broad

155

Welcoming Rifugio Genova is worth the detour

In either case the views are stunning and range for 360 degrees, taking in a vast selection of Dolomites as well as the northern snow-capped Austrian Alps.

saddle (2760m) you have two choices: the first is to tackle the final cable-aided stretch via an exposed shoulder for the last 150m hands-on climb to the summit of **Sass de Putia** (2875m, **1hr 20min**). Should that not appeal, turn L (W) at the saddle for the easy route to the twin peak, **Piccolo Sass de Putia**, only a matter of metres lower! ◀

Return the same way to **Forcella di Putia** (**40min**) and fork sharp L. Path n.35 drops easily over pasture slopes rife with marmots, soon joined by the variant route from Rifugio Genova. A white gravel lane takes over as you head NE through the manicured pasture of Pra de Putia, past scattered timber huts used at haymaking time. One of these, **Ütia Vaciara** (2025m), has been tastefully converted into a rustic eatery with a splendid outlook over Val Badia to Sasso della Croce. ◀ Soon afterwards you keep L (NE) diagonally uphill through light wood and flowered slopes, to the minor pass **Göma** (2111m, **1hr**), marked by a crucifix and playful wooden sculptures.

On this open terrain chances are good of spotting soaring birds of prey.

The path from Forcella Putia wanders through meadows dotted with haymaking huts

Next is a drop L (NW) on n.8A, with views down to the village of Antermoia. The shady wood that follows provides shelter for both black grouse and capercaillie, attracted by the laden bilberry bushes in late summer. Pastureland featuring tall purple gentians follows, then, after a short stretch of dirt track, you keep L via another inviting refreshment stop, **Ütia de Göma** (2036m). Heading due W now, you plunge into wood that has grown up amid huge fallen boulders directly below the main peak, the walls of which rise vertiginously overhead. The path climbs out back to pasture and the farm-cum-snack bar **Munt de Funella**, in the vicinity of the 2067m junction encountered on the outward section. Turn R to return to **Passo delle Erbe** (**1hr 30min**).

WALK 30
Sentiero delle Odle

Start/Finish	Ranui, upper Val di Funes
Distance	17km
Ascent/Descent	950m
Grade	2
Walking time	5hr (4hr 20min with return bus from Rifugio Zannes)
Maps	Tabacco n.05 or n.030 scale 1:25,000
Refreshments	Rifugio Malga Brogles, Glatschalm, Rifugio Zannes
Access	Ranui (near S Maddalena) has year-round SAD buses. In summer the line is extended to Rifugio Zannes and its car park – handy for the return.

The Sentiero delle Odle (Adolf Munkel Weg in German) is justifiably renowned as one of the most beautiful walking routes in the whole of the Dolomites. Named after the founder of the Dresden Alpine Club, it is a delightful wander between the 1900m and 2000m mark, giving walkers ample time to drink in the marvellous scenery. It skirts the base of the spectacular Odle, a perfectly suited name that means 'needles' in Ladin. Countless soaring spires and jagged teeth rise to dizzy heights above vast scree flows, while the valley flanks are cloaked with dense, dark green forests of conifer.

The Odle group blocks off the head of Val di Funes, a particularly peaceful rural valley. Its high-altitude summer farms all occupy marvellous positions and supplement their income by serving meals and taking in guests, a boon for visitors. The walk described here begins on forestry and farm tracks, while clearly marked paths across pasture and scree account for the high-altitude sections. In good weather there is no difficulty, but it does rate average in combined terms of fatigue and duration. Autumn, when the larch trees turn golden, can be particularly stunning.

From the modest hamlet of Ranui (1346m) ▶ and its well-kept meadows, take the narrowing road (n.28) lined with hedgerows to a parking area with a café-resto, and start of a forestry track (closed to unauthorised traffic). Not far along this veers R (S) to continue in shady wood alongside the Kliefer Bach. Further along you criss-cross the stream and climb to a junction where the track comes to an end. Keep R still on path n.28 which now starts labouring seriously up through light conifer wood and past a waterfall. Quite close to the foot of the inspiring Odle, at a **fork** (1899m) turn R onto n.35 for the remaining short stretch to **Rifugio Malga Brogles** (2045m, **2hr15min**). ▶

The late Baroque church of St Johann from 1744, with an onion-domed bell tower, is nearby.

This working dairy farm doubles as a restaurant for visitors, who can also reach it from Val Gardena (see Walk 31).

Rifugio Malga Brogles and the Odle – what a beautiful combination

Fossils are common along the Sentiero delle Odle

Backtrack to the **fork** then proceed NE on n.35, the Sentiero delle Odle. ▶ Ignore the fork for Forcella Pana and drop through a clearing followed by spreads of dwarf pines, where the path becomes white gravel. After the turn-off for Forcella di Mesdì, you climb an eroding earth ridge (2017m) and pass forks to unpronounceable Gschnagenhardt Alm, not far below in a star-shaped clearing – a possible exit route. Now you are directly beneath magnificent, neck-craning 3025m Sass Rigais. On the ensuing stretch the path twists and turns to avoid fallen boulders and tracts where scree flows encroach. Beneath the next easily recognisable tooth-like point, Furchetta (fork), you come to the key **junction** (1993m, **1hr 30min**), where you turn L on n.36 and leave the rocky realms of the Sentiero delle Odle to move into pastoral surrounds. Beautifully placed **Glatschalm** (1902m, **15min**), a short distance downhill, is a typical summer farm. ▶

A wide farm track (n.36) leads in leisurely curves N down to the clutch of restaurants and guesthouses that includes **Rifugio Zannes** (1685m, **20min**), as well as a

Along with pretty banks of pink alpenrose, there is woodland of larch and Arolla pine that shelters timid roe deer.

The flowered meadows are quite a sight!

bus stop and information centre. Unless you jump on a bus for Ranui, you'll need forestry track n.33, which heads due W on the southern edge of the Schwarzwald (Black Forest). Where the track bears L (S), a path breaks off straight ahead to hug the banks of Rio di Funes, and it is a delightful stroll. This leads back to the farm track at the start of the walk. Keep R for the short distance back to **Ranui** (**40min**).

WALK 31
The Rasciesa Ridge

Start/Finish	Main square, Ortisei
Distance	17.5km (14km if you return via cable car)
Ascent	280m
Descent	900m
Grade	1–2
Walking time	4hr 45min (3hr 45min if you return via cable car)
Map	Tabacco n.05 scale 1:25,000
Refreshments	Ortisei, Baita Resciesa, Rifugio Resciesa, Rifugio Malga Brogles, Caffè Martin
Access	Ortisei has year-round SAD buses. The bus stops are in the main square, Piazza San Antonio.

The Rasciesa (or Resciesa) is a gently inclined plateau that culminates in a jagged 2300m crest and dominates Ortisei. It acts as the dividing line between Ladin-speaking Val Gardena and German-speaking Val di Funes to the north. Compared to its neighbour – the stunning Odle group – it is unspectacular, but it makes up for this with incredible wide-ranging views.

This walk begins with an enjoyable ride on a state-of-the-art funicular railway, which replaced the historic chairlift. Then comes a panoramic traverse via inviting eateries that also offer accommodation, followed by a drawn-out but not particularly steep descent (which can be reduced by 650m/1hr thanks to a gondola lift).

From Ortisei's (1236m) main square and its elaborate Baroque church, follow signs uphill on a series of escalators to the base of the Seceda *funivia* lift (you return here later). Now it's a walk L for **10min** up to the Rasciesa *funicolare* (**funicular**). The mechanised cabins glide up the forested slope, home to many a squawking nutcracker. When you disembark at **Baita Resciesa** (2050m), take wide paved path n.35A. It quickly joins n.35 heading W across the grassy hillside carpeted with juniper shrubs and heather, where cows and chestnut Haflinger horses graze freely to where **Rifugio Resciesa** (2165m) stands in a lovely open spot.

From the Resciesa ridge the views northeast take in Rifugio Resciesa as well as the Sella massif and Sassolungo

The path continues to Santa Croce chapel on the westernmost extremity of the plateau. Here turn uphill to **Auserraschötz** aka Mont Dedora (2281m, **45min**) and its masterpiece sculpted wooden crucifix with a larger-than-life Christ. ▶

The isolated position is enjoys fantastic 360-degree views embracing the snowbound Austrian Alps and masses of Dolomites.

A clear but narrow path (n.10) leads E along the crest then diagonally down through pasture studded with fat gentians and black vanilla orchids to join n.31 (a direct route from the funicular). Hillsides wooded with Arolla

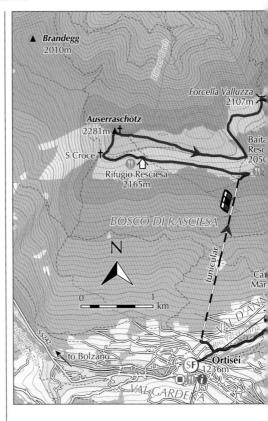

This stretch affords exceptional views of the Odle rock needles and scree flows, and the exposed rock and earth layers of the massive Seceda.

pines, alpenrose and juniper characterise the stretch swinging round to a bench and cross at **Forcella Valluzza** aka Flitzerscharte (2107m). A little further on, you join a wide track, continuing E. ◄

From the broad saddle of Passo di Brogles (2119m), it's a short downhill stroll to Rifugio Malga Brogles (2045m, **1hr 45min**). ◄

This summer farm doubles as a walkers' refuge and modest summer eatery.

Back up at **Passo di Brogles**, branch L (SW) on path n.5 to head downhill. The path follows a stream, enters conifer wood then takes a red earth-rock crest, with good

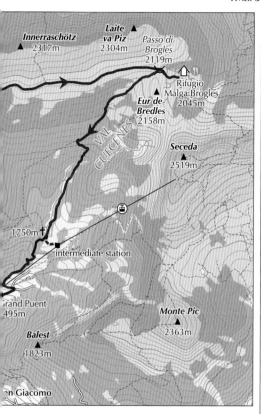

views of the Seceda strata. Further down, it traverses the bed of the broad watercourse Cuecenes, not long before a signed junction and **crucifix** (1750m, **1hr**). ▶

Exit to lift (10min): to bail out here, take the path L (E) to the intermediate station, where you can catch the gondola lift and return to Ortisei.

THE SECEDA

The Seceda is of great interest to geology enthusiasts as multi-layered beds underlying the Dolomites' original coral deposits are exposed. The most ancient is a blood-red sandstone dating back over 250 million years and rich in fossils; in 1969 it yielded vertebrae and bone fragments belonging to a porpoise-like Ichthyosaurus. This is overlaid with multitudinous grey-white chalks while a wine-red porphyry from a later, volcanic phase is also visible further downhill. Special finds are on display at the Ortisei museum www. museumgherdeina.it/en.

Approaching Passo di Brogles while admiring the Odle

Keep straight on, passing under the cables to reach an old house and mill on a road. On the tarmac you walk down to cross a marvellous old timber bridge, **Grand Puent** (1495m), over a curious mini-canyon gouged out of a thick bed of red porphyry rock. There is a road junction and **Caffè Martin** nearby, where you fork L on the path signed for Val d'Anna, with great views to interesting strata on the Balest, southeast across the valley. A steep

drop brings you to another café ensconced in the wood. A delightful path back and forth acrosssm the stream passes picnic and play areas, finally reaching the arrival station of the gondola lift. As per the walk start, take the escalators back to the village and **main square** of Ortisei (**1hr 15min**), where you began.

ORTISEI

That remarkable animal on a little wheeled platform which we fondly took to represent a horse ... he is of the purest Grödner Thal breed. Those wooden-jointed dolls of all sizes, from babies half an inch in length to mothers of families two feet high, whose complexions always came off when we washed their faces ... all the cheap, familiar, absurd treasures of your earliest childhood and of mine – they all came, Reader, from St. Ulrich!

Amelia Edwards (1873)

Artistic woodcarving has long been a mainstay in the burgeoning town of Ortisei/St Ulrich in Val Gardena/Grödner Thal, 'the capital of Toyland' for Amelia Edwards. The woodcarvers' raw material is the Arolla pine which grow in abundance alongside pasture on the Rasciesa.

WALK 32

*Across the
Puez-Odle Altopiano*

Start/Finish	Dantercepies gondola lift station, Selva di Val Gardena
Distance	16km
Ascent	500m
Descent	1150m
Grade	2
Walking time	5hr
Maps	Tabacco n.07 and 05 scale 1:25,000
Refreshments	Selva, Dantercepies, Jimmy's Hütte, Rifugio Puez
Access	Selva has year-round SAD buses and a summer service continues to the Dantercepies gondola lift.

This exciting and rewarding walk takes you into the very heart of the Puez-Odle group. A gondola lift is used for the initial 700m of ascent, followed by a series of short climbs and descents, before a final 800m drop via the magnificent Vallunga (long valley), a textbook example of a U-shaped, glacially formed, trough valley. Plenty of drinking water is a must, and sun protection gear is recommended, as there is almost no shade. A manned hut, Rifugio Puez, lies halfway, perfect for lunch unless you opt for a picnic.

PUEZ-ODLE GROUP

The rambling Puez-Odle group and nature park accounts for the mountainous corner between Val Gardena and Val Badia. It features an elevated central plateau that averages 2400m in altitude and hosts pasture basins smothered with wildflowers. It is not as crowded as the neighbouring Sella group, improving chances of seeing chamois, and maybe even one of the legendary dragons that reputedly slumber in the depths of the rare scattered lakes. In actual fact surface water is unusual here due to widespread karstification.

Other delights to look out for are the rock slabs laid bare by erosion and embedded with fossilised Megalodont shells. Resembling cleft hoofprints of deer (or the devil!), these bivalve shells – averaging 10cm in length – are at least around 200 million years old. Lastly are the volcanic-looking cones that punctuate the central plateau – solitary remnants of the Jurassic and Cretaceous layers that once covered the whole area, reminiscent of Monument Valley.

There are brilliant views across to the magnificent Sella massif, and over to the Lagazuoi and Tofane. ◄

At Selva, from the lower Dantercepies *cabinovia* station (1645m) ride up to the uppermost station **Dantercepies** (2295m). A short way uphill near the Mountain Lounge restaurant turn R (E), to coast along the base of the Gran Cir over grassy slopes thick with purple asters and gentians. ◄

At the snack bar **Jimmy's Hütte** (2222m) branch L into the Puez-Odle Nature Park, embarking on a steady NE climb through low-lying mountain pines and bleached rock. You soon gain a silent inner valley, host to a jungle of bizarre knobbly rock pinnacles. Further up is **Passo Cir** (2469m, **40min**). A sheep gate then leads

The rocky path at Passo Cir

to a drop NE (ignore the turn-off for Selva) as you cut across the head of barren Val de Chedul and up to **Passo Crespeina** (2530m, **15min**), and its evocative sculpted crucifix. The marvellous views here take in the Sciliar and Sassopiatto-Sassolungo and the vast spread of the undulating innermost Puez plateau.

The path descends gently NE and passes **Lago di Crespeina** (2374m), which has perfect shores for leisurely daytime picnics. ▶

The ensuing stretch traverses huge 45-degree tilted rock strata, en route to yet another pass, **Forcella de Ciampac** (2366m). A brief rock corridor reinforced with timber treads leads N over the plateau below one of the curious cones, Somafurcia, and over broad rock slabs embedded with fossilised shells. ▶ After a flagpole is welcoming **Rifugio Puez** (2475m, **1hr 20min**), backed by another strange green-red peak, Col de Puez. A restorative pause and a slice of luscious Apfelstrudel are in order here.

Then you need to take n.14 due S for the plunge into Vallunga. The path is good, if steep at times, and is

After nightfall, however, a halt is inadvisable due to the danger of flaming red mice plunging into the waters, according to local lore!

You walk past the head of magnificent Vallunga, its perfect U-shape clearly recognisable. Punta Santner and the Sciliar appear at its far extremity.

169

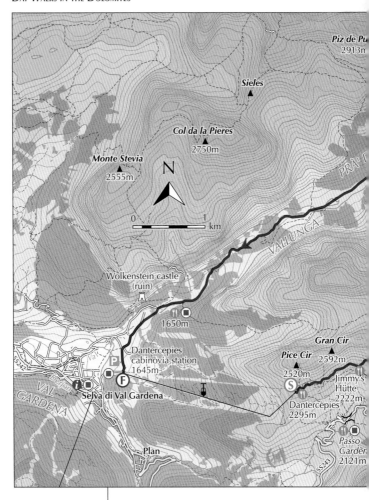

flanked by masses of felt-petalled edelweiss and scrubby vegetation that anchors the loose terrain. Down at the bottom, at a white rubble gully and stream, you cross to the R side of the valley below towering cliffs, the bulk of

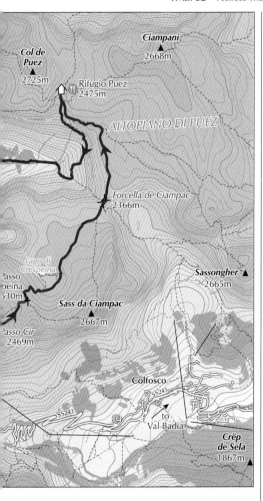

the descent now behind you. The path heads W below a waterfall through larch trees.

The beautiful pasture flat **Prà da Ri** (1800m) is not far further along. ▶ A hut marks the start of a *via crucis*,

Meaning 'meadow for laughing', it was the site of merrymaking and fancy dress parties for the gentry of Selva in olden times.

171

with artistic stations of the cross accompanying the broad gravel lane through light wood from here on. Later on you'll glimpse the ruins of Wolkenstein Castle high above. Erected in the 1200s, it was short-lived due to damaging rockfalls; only a couple of walls are left standing.

The lane concludes at the **Vallunga car park** with a café and bus stop (1650m, **2hr 30min**). If you don't opt for the bus back to Selva, keep straight ahead through to the Carabinieri training premises, then turn L down to the gondola lift station (**15min**) where you started out.

WALK 33
The Bullaccia Tour

Start/Finish	Gondola lift arrival station, Compaccio
Distance	8.8km (7.8km if you ride the Bullaccia lift)
Ascent/Descent	380m (130m if you ride the Bullaccia lift)
Grade	1
Walking time	3hr (2hr 15min if you ride the Bullaccia lift)
Map	Tabacco n.05 scale 1:25,000
Refreshments	Compaccio, Tschötsch, Berggasthof Puflatsch, Arnikahütte, Dibaita Puflatsch Hütte
Access	Compaccio is reached by gondola lift from Siusi, in turn served by SAD buses. The road from Siusi up to Compaccio can only be used by guests of Alpe di Siusi accommodation.

This popular walk, the Bullaccia Tour aka Puflatsch Umrundung (abbreviated PU) ensures a rewarding outing, suitable for all. Wildlife sightings are not unusual, as chamois enjoy early summer grazing, and birds of prey may be spotted circling over the pastures. Wildflowers such as wine-red martagon lilies and scented pinks are common in summer.

Along the way a string of manned huts-cum-restaurants offer meals and refreshments, though a small grocery shop at Compaccio/Kompatsch does picnic supplies. At the walk start, the Bullaccia lift means a saving of 45min/250m in ascent for the lazy.

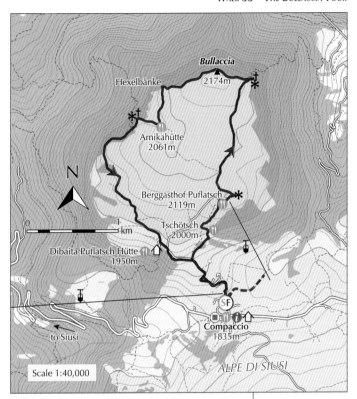

BULLACCIA

Up on the rolling high-altitude Alpe di Siusi/Seiser Alm, the Bullaccia/
Puflatsch (also spelt Bulacia) slopes off northwards, an apparently insignifi-
cant slab that culminates in a 2174m hummock. However the mountain was
infamous in the past, especially during the late Middle Ages when rumours
and hysteria were rife of witches meeting there as well as on the nearby
Sciliar. Even earlier it was a lookout for Roman sentries, thanks to its bird's-
eye observation points. Brilliant views remain its great draw card, appreciated by summer strollers and winter skiers alike.

The Berggasthof Puflatsch is a scenic spot

At your feet spreads Val Gardena, backed by the Puez-Odle with the Seceda outcrop and Rasciesa ridge. Sassopiatto-Sassolungo, flanked by the terraced Sella, dominate to the southeast.

From the Compaccio gondola lift arrival (1835m), turn L for n.14, up the steep road past hotels and through fields. Soon after a winter ski station, path n.14/PU branches R (NE) across a grassy piste climbing easily through woodland and up to the café **Tschötsch** (2000m), beautifully placed if unpronounceable. You cut across a lane and continue up to **Berggasthof Puflatsch** (2119m, **45min**), and the arrival of a gondola lift. A wonderfully scenic spot – though much, much more is promised!

Signs point R to a **lookout** (*piattaforma panoramica*) with labelled mountain profiles – quite stunning! It is also known as Engelrast for its artistic angel atop a pole.

Here take the path L to join the lane (PU) heading R (NNE). This leisurely amble with gentle ups and downs, leads to the northeastern corner of the Bullaccia and a **crucifix** in a breathtaking position on the brink of a vertiginous drop! ◀

Next, PU follows the cliff edge W above Arolla pines which have colonised the cliffs. You pass the modest **Bullaccia peak** (2174m) without noticing it, en route to the curious **Hexelbänke**. ▸

Press on down wooden steps in gentle descent through flowered grassy terrain. After a cross the path veers L to friendly **Arnikahütte** (2061m, **1hr**). (From here a lane cuts SW back to the gondola lift in 20min if needed.)

Now PU turns uphill R to a huge **cross** and picnic table high above Castelrotto. It then narrows as it follows the cliff edge through low shrubs and conifers, a magnificent stretch. You join a lane past summer huts and gain a rise. Stick with PU and head over to the access ramp for superbly placed eatery **Dibaita Puflatsch Hütte** (1950m), with a vast outlook stretching from the Sciliar to the snow-capped Austrian Alps. Another wonderful spot.

A broad track in decisive descent takes you back down to the **gondola lift** at **Compaccio** (**1hr 15min**).

The 'witches' benches' as legend would have it, are in actual fact square-angled columns of volcanic augite porphyry.

WALK 34
Alpe di Siusi Circuit and Rifugio Bolzano

Start/Finish	Tourist Office, Compaccio
Distance	11.5km (+6km for extension to Rifugio Bolzano)
Ascent/Descent	500m (+550m for extension to Rifugio Bolzano)
Grade	2
Walking time	3hr 10min (+2hr 30min for extension to Rifugio Bolzano)
Maps	Tabacco n.05 or 029 scale 1:25,000
Refreshments	Compaccio, Prossliner Schwaige, Rifugio Bolzano, Saltnerhütte, Hotel Panorama
Access	Compaccio is reached by gondola lift from Siusi, in turn served by SAD buses. The road from Siusi up to Compaccio can only be used by guests of Alpe di Siusi accommodation. The Tourist Office is on the main road, 5min from the gondola lift.

Spectacular and straightforward, this rewarding loop walk follows clearly marked paths through varied landscapes with superb views. The PeakFinder app is very helpful today. On the outward leg the Sciliar and dramatic cleft Punta Santner (named after local mountaineer Johann Santer, who first scaled it in 1880) steal the show, whereas the return is dominated by the magnificent Sassopiatto-Sassolungo. Fit walkers should plan on including the extension to Rifugio Bolzano – making a total of 5hr 40min.

Should you not opt for a panoramic picnic (Compaccio has a grocery shop), the huts en route all serve meals, snacks and all manner of drinks, and often double as venues for rollicking live music, Tyrolian style.

ALPE DI SIUSI

Ranging from 1700m above sea level to the 2000m mark, the glorious Alpe di Siusi spells vast rolling meadows that even in this day and age continue to function as pasture and haymaking arena for the village of Siusi, located 1000m below at a much lower, more liveable altitude. Cows, sheep and attractive red-tan Haflinger horses with blond manes graze here.

The Alpe is dominated by an ancient coral reef known as the Sciliar/Schlern. Volcanic intrusions at its base have encouraged the growth of lush pasture, which is carpeted with an unbelievable array of wild flowers and fed by plentiful springs and streams draining off the mountain. It comes under the 64km^2 Parco Naturale dello Sciliar, heaven for summer walkers as well as a winter paradise for cross-country skiers. You can wander in peace for days amongst dark timber farm chalets and summer farms, many doubling as picturesque cafés. Beethoven's *Pastoral* comes easily to mind.

Alongside the Compaccio (1835m) tourist office and a board listing the huts ahead, you need the minor road labelled Joch. Take wide path n.10 that breaks off R after the first bend. It heads SW across meadows with old timber chalets and vast views including the snowbound Austrian Alps shimmering in the north, while the imposing Sciliar massif stands out west.

You cross a dirt road (1957m) connecting the Spitzbühel and Panorama chairlifts, and keep straight ahead down to another path junction looking over to the

Autumn colours on the crest prior to Prossliner Schwaige

striking Terrarossa teeth-like points SE. Ignore the lane L and stick with n.10. Here it is a narrow path via a scenic crest smothered with martagon lilies and larch trees. Down at a farm lane keep R for delightful **Prossliner Schwaige** (1740m) on the edge of a chasm at the foot of awesome Punta Santner.

Branch L cutting SE below meadows and into tree cover to cross a series of bridges and cascading streams where striking geological layers of limestone and volcanic rock are revealed. You pass a fork L (a handy short cut to Saltnerhütte if needed) and follow n.10 over more streams and strata before a zigzagging climb through conifers. Ignore the n.1A branch (R) and continue up to a clearing and path **junction** (1900m, **1hr 40min**) and the optional extension to Rifugio Bolzano.

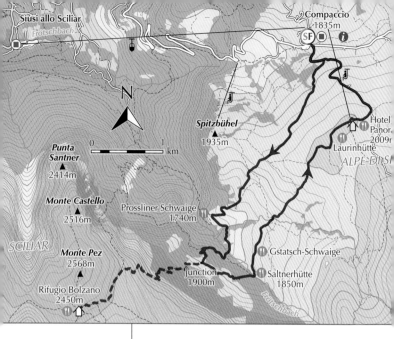

Extension to Rifugio Bolzano (2hr 30min return)

Take a deep breath and turn R to embark on well-trodden n.1 with its seemingly interminable zigzags. The imposing rock barrier is eventually climbed and the reward a magnificent undulating high-altitude plateau, the Altopiano dello Sciliar, with superb views of the neighbouring Catinaccio range and much beyond. In pale stone, old fashioned **Rifugio Bolzano** (2450m), dating back to 1885, has a marvellous glassed-in dining area and easily ranks high among the best-placed huts in the Dolomites. Suitably refreshed, retrace your steps to the 1900m **junction** afterwards to pick up the main route.

Main route

The owners promote it as the 'letzte Tankstelle' (last filling station) before the Sciliar ascent.

At the 1900m junction go L for the gentle descent through Arolla pines and lacy larch, and across a bridge to welcoming summer eatery **Saltnerhütte** (1850m). ◀ Here a wide lane leads past another café-farm (**Gstatsch-Schwaige**) to a bridge where path n.6

breaks off R. This climbs via lush pasture slopes and touches on farms. ▶ Cross a lane for a wooden walkway over marshy terrain via Laurinhütte and a lift, and on to **Hotel Panorama** (2009m, **1hr**). Café-restaurant, orientation table, chairlift.

All that's left to do now is head over to the minor road that winds its leisurely way NW back down to **Compaccio** (**30min**).

There are gorgeous views of Sassopiatto-Sassolungo to the east. Where the gradient eases, so much comes into view that you'll need the PeakFinder app!

WALK 35
Castel Presule

Start/Finish	Tourist Office, Fiè (on the main road, near the bus stops)
Distance	7.5km (4.5km if returning to Fiè via bus)
Ascent/Descent	325m (125m if returning to Fiè via bus)
Grade	1
Time	2hr 20min (1hr 35min if returning to Fiè via bus) +1hr for the castle visit
Map	Tabacco n.029 scale 1:25,000
Refreshments	Fiè, Umser Mühlele, Castel Presule
Access	Fiè is served year-round by frequent SAD buses on the Bolzano–Castelrotto line, as well as the rare run from Tires via Presule.

This delightful wander heads out from the historic village of Fiè/Völs through meadows and traditional farms occupying the vast slopes that climb up to the dark forested mountainsides and sheer rock flanks of the monumental Sciliar massif. The destination Castel Presule/Schloss Prösels, makes for a fascinating visit and is a rare treat for the Dolomites. The low altitude (800–900m above sea level) makes the walk feasible from spring through to autumn. The route is dotted with well-kept shrines and panoramic benches, and refreshments can be had at the castle café.

From the Tourist Office at Fiè (880m) follow the main road for 350 metres in the direction of Bolzano, to

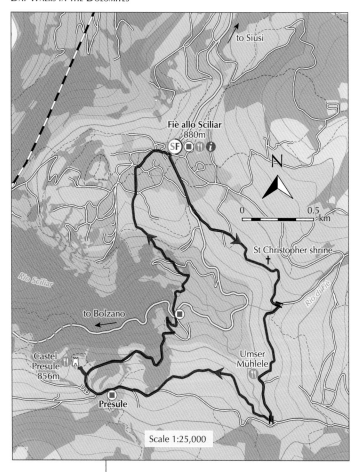

The village of Presule comes into view ahead, its castle on an isolated outcrop in a commanding position.

where quiet farm road, Christophbildweg (n.6), turns off L. Heading SE it is lined with grape vines and apple orchards. Up at T-junction fork R onto an unsurfaced lane past the **St Christopher shrine** that gave the lane its name. ◀ Hedgerows and shady walnut trees line the way through fields and well-kept farms.

Marvellous Castel Presule and its cafè

After crossing a bridge over a stream, turn R, still on n.6 mostly S around hillsides. Down at **Umser Mühlele** café-restaurant a minor road leads up past a cluster of houses to another bridge. Here it's R – on n.3 now – for a delightful stroll through woodland and farms with wide-ranging views back to Fiè and the Renon plateau beyond. Up at tarmac turn R through to the quiet village of **Presule** with a 12th-century square brick guard tower, the Pulverturm. Not far downhill at a restaurant, keep R for superbly photogenic **Castel Presule** (856m, **1hr 15min**), complete with picnic area and café.

CASTEL PRESULE

The earliest part of the castle dates back to the 1100s, but it was in the 1500s under Leonhard von Völs, governor of Südtirol, that the medieval building really took shape. It was fitted with an outer wall and towers, state-of-the-art fortifications, chapel, underground water storage, frescoed loggia, elegant living quarters with decorated timber ceilings and a great hall. Not to mention a dungeon prison with one-way access – an eight metre drop. More darkness dates back to this time as a frenzy of witch-hunting and 'trials' followed by cruel torture were held here. Nine women from Fiè alone were condemned to death. Charges of alleged 'evildoing' ranged from cohabitation with the devil, rain-making and riding on broomsticks, to slaying unborn children and denial of the Catholic faith.

The castle is open for guided visits May–October, daily except Saturday. Tours are conducted in German and Italian, with an audio guide for English and French. https://schloss-proesels.seiseralm.it tel 0471 601062.

The castle looks towards the Sciliar

By all means take the bus back to Fiè.

However do find time for an exploratory wander through the charming upper historic part of the village with its old inns and imposing Baroque church.

After the fascinating visit, follow the narrow road downhill NE for 1km to where a lane (n.5) branches L. It narrows to a path through chestnut wood, dropping via a field to the main road and **bus stop** (**20min**). ◄

N.5 dips under the road to continue straight down past a farm to a bridged stream. Keep L and uphill – at times puffingly steeply – on lanes and paved paths touching on mountainside farms. Once you reach meadows, tarmac and a T-junction with an 1828 shrine, keep L then immediately R. This leads around the edge of **Fiè**, and through to the main road where you began (**45min**). ◄

WALK 36
Val Ciamin

Start/Finish	Bus stop, San Cipriano
Distance	11km (+7km for extension to Rifugio Bergamo)
Ascent/Descent	570m (+550m for extension to Rifugio Bergamo)
Grade	1–2
Walking time	4hr (+2hr 20min for extension to Rifugio Bergamo)
Maps	Tabacco n.029, n.06 or n.05 scale 1:25,000
Refreshments	San Cipriano, Tschamin Schwaige, Rifugio Bergamo
Access	SAD buses from Bolzano via Tires reach San Cipriano. A run from Paolina (near Passo di Costalunga) also comes this far.

Located in the Parco Naturale Sciliar-Catinaccio, Val Ciamin is the easternmost arm of Val di Tires, and is a wild river canyon that slices into the marvellous Catinaccio massif and terminates abruptly under the Antermoia outcrop.

This is a delightful stroll on good paths and forestry lanes exploring a heavily wooded valley – it took a battering from the 2018 storm Vaia, but the trees are growing back at an encouraging rate. Numerous natural springs occur en route.

In the upper valley an optional extension (an additional 2hr 20min return) climbs to beautifully placed Rifugio Bergamo.

In San Cipriano (1080m) from the **bus stop** opposite the Zyprianerhof hotel, follow signs downhill for n.4A. It soon forks R around a field then drops to houses and tarmac. Stay with it to the nearby valley floor where you go R along the gushing stream in Val Ciamin.

Not far on you cross a footbridge to a path junction – and turn R on n.3. After a second bridge the path climbs with steps through undergrowth bright with flowers, such as wine-red columbines. Up at a lane, fork L to the Tschamin Schwaige café and neighbouring Steger Säge sawmill aka **Park Visitor Centre** (1140m, **30min**).

PARK VISITOR CENTRE

The informative Visitor Centre for the Parco Naturale dello Sciliar-Catinaccio occupies a showcase Venetian-style sawmill that dates back 400 years and shows the importance of woodcutting here over the centuries. It is powered by water from the adjacent mountain stream and, amazingly, is still in working order.

Well-trodden path n.3 now heads decidedly uphill through beautiful conifer wood brightened with alpenrose shrubs. Far below is the stream rushing under dizzy, sheer cliffs.

About half an hour up you join a forestry lane and go L past a **crucifix**. Not far along is the first of two springs. Heading E the track crosses the watercourse several times. After a clearing, Schlaferter Leger (1487m), continue on to the spectacular meadow, **Rechter Leger**

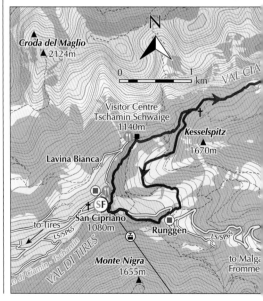

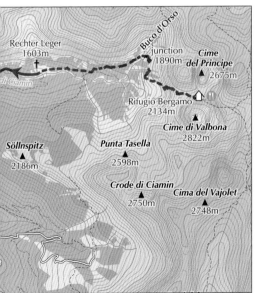

Rechter Leger is a great scenic picnic spot

The magnificent outlook includes Crode di Ciamin and Cime di Valbona beyond dark tree cover, while on a grassy ledge below Cime del Principe, the flag of Rifugio Bergamo is just visible.

(1603m, **1hr 45min**) complete with hut and crucifix, the perfect picnic spot. ◀

Extension to Rifugio Bergamo (2hr 20min return)

The clear path continues E, soon branching L (ENE) in more decided ascent through wood. It enters the wild, white gully of **Buco d'Orso** (bear's hole!), where walkers are dwarfed by the Cime del Principe. At a **junction** (1890m, **40min**), ignore path n.3A and fork R to cut up through wood along the rocky flanks of Grasleitental. Hospitable **Rifugio Bergamo** (2134m, **50min**) occupies a wonderful perch, worlds away from it all. Return to Rechter Leger afterwards.

Main route

Once your senses are saturated, backtrack down Val Ciamin. At the **crucifix** after the springs, ignore the turn-off for the Visitor Centre and stay on the forestry track. Mostly SW, it curves round the hillsides, soon cutting through sweet-smelling meadows alive with bees frantically harvesting pollen from the masses of gorgeous blooms. Modest timber hay chalets are dotted over the slopes. Soon peeping over the hill, and improving little by little, is the exceptional backdrop of the resplendent Catinaccio with its fairy-tale towers.

Back in woodland, ignore the fork for n.12 but not far after it turn R off the lane for the path cutting down to the road and bus stop at **Runggen**. If you don't catch the bus here to return to the walk start, take the narrow path (n.3) that plunges through wood, parallel to the road. It joins a lane which brings you out at **San Cipriano** (**1hr 45min**).

WALK 37

The Inner Catinaccio

Start/Finish	Rifugio Ciampediè
Distance	12.5km (+4.2km for extension)
Ascent/Descent	810m (+700m for extension)
Grade	3 (2 for extension)
Walking time	5hr (+1hr 45min for extension)
Maps	Tabacco n.029 or n.06 scale 1:25,000
Refreshments	Rifugio Ciampediè, Rifugio Nigritella, Rifugio Gardeccia, Rifugio Stella Alpina, Rifugio Vaiolet, Rifugio Preuss, Rifugio Passo Principe, Rifugio Re Alberto, Rifugio Passo Santner
Access	Rifugio Ciampediè can be reached by cable car from Vigo di Fassa, or a series of chairlifts from Pera di Fassa. Val di Fassa itself has Trentino Trasporti buses from Trento, and SAD runs from Bolzano via Passo di Costalunga.

Clearly visible from Bolzano railway station, this celebrated Dolomite group is known in Italian as the Catinaccio, from 'large basin' or 'bowl' for its open shell-shaped formation. Its breathtaking rock spires have long attracted mountaineers, naturally. The first recorded ascent of the highest point, the 3004m Catinaccio d'Antermoia, dates back to 1872, with the various Torri del Vaiolet following.

The walk described here ventures into the dizzy rocky reaches of the spectacular Catinaccio, touching on well-run huts that cater to multitudes of summer walkers. After an easy path entering the marvellous Catinaccio to a series of refuges, it tackles a steep gully leading to a breathtaking amphiteatre and lookout. While not particularly exposed, it does mean a challenging hands-on clamber, and is unsuitable for inexperienced walkers. Naturally, it will feel more exposed on the way back down. Do not embark on this route in unsettled weather, as the iron fittings could attract lightning. An easier alternative extension to Passo Principe is given.

It stands just inside the open southern edge of the Catinaccio, an amazing spot to start as the outlook embraces most of the group's awesome peaks.

The cable car arrival is close to old-style Rifugio Ciampediè (1997m), from the Ladin for 'field of God'. ◄

Take path n.540, heading W at first past **Rifugio Negritella** before a saunter NW through light woods of larch, alpenrose and juniper – home to shy roe deer. Take a good look at breathtaking Dirupi di Larsec and Cima Catinaccio, and soaring Torri del Vaiolet. Further on is **Rifugio Gardeccia** (1950m, **40min**) along with a cluster of modest shops selling souvenirs and groceries.

Popular route n.546, a jeep-width track N, passes Rifugio Stella Alpina and the last of the trees before climbing into the rock-dominated landscape, where myriad wild flowers stand out against the bleached stones. You tackle the tall rock barrier across the valley in wide curves that take the sting out of the otherwise very steep climb. You emerge on a platform at Rifugio Preuss, next door to the rambling and beautifully renovated historic **Rifugio Vaiolet** (2243m, **50min**), its curious name derived from the ancient Ladin for 'cleft' or 'split', describing the rock towers.

Extension to Passo Principe (1hr 45min return)

Walkers who make an early start have a good chance of meeting staff ferrying supplies by mechanised wheelbarrow to the hut further up.

From **Rifugio Vaiolet** (2243m), well-trodden path n.584 leads N and follows the broad innermost valley of the Catinaccio, **Val del Vaiolet**. ◄ It's an inspiring walk beneath a superb procession of soaring rock points to **Passo Principe** (2599m, **1hr**), where the eponymous refuge perches, apparently precariously, under Cima Valbona.

Punta Ta
2598r

Crode
2

Rifugio
Passo
Santner
2741m

Ci
Catin
298

Cima Coron
2797m

Cima Sforcel
2810m ▲

Teston dal Vaje
2646m ▲

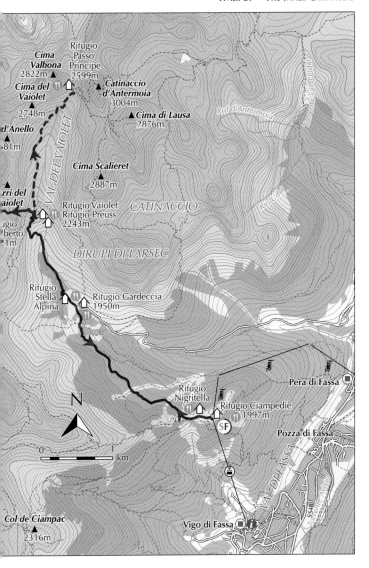

A clear path climbs to Passo Principe

However, your attention will immediately be taken by the solid mass of the neighbouring Catinaccio d'Antermoia, which rises to 3004m above a huge scree-filled amphitheatre. Return to **Rifugio Vaiolet** the same way (**45min**).

Main route

From **Rifugio Vaiolet** (2243m), take n.542 due W up the broad rocky gully beneath the cable for the refuges' goods lift. Clearly marked with red painted arrows and stripes, the path zigzags up the steep rock flank to the first of several long tracts of well-anchored cable, to be tackled with due care. A trickling stream keeps you company, as do some startlingly colourful rock flowers.

After 400m of ascent you enter a silent, lunar-like amphitheatre with a diminutive snow-melt lake and crowned by majestic towers. Known as the Gartl, it is both unworldly and magical. It hosts **Rifugio Re Alberto** (2621m, **1hr**), named in honour of Belgian King Albert I, who scaled numerous peaks in the company of local expert guide Tita Piaz in the early 1900s. Strategically situated for the rock climbers who throng here, it is placed directly at the foot of three dizzy spires of the Torri del Vaiolet: (L to R) Torre Delago, named after the Innsbruck climber who first reached the 2780m top in 1895; Torre Stabele, for the Tyrolean guide who scaled its 2805m in 1892; and Torre Winkler, in memory of the intrepid 18-year-old student who climbed solo to the 2800m point in 1887. ▶

Film buffs will recognise the towers from the opening sequence of *Cliffhanger* (1992).

Continue uphill on n.542, which curves SW to head for stunning Passo Santner (2741m), located between Cima Catinaccio and Croda di Re Laurino. Space-age **Rifugio Passo Santner** (**15min**) is perched on the plunging western edge of the Catinaccio. ▶

When you've had your fill of views, backtrack with care down to **Rifugio Vaiolet** (**1hr**). Finally, return to **Rifugio Gardeccia** (**35min**) and on to **Rifugio Ciampediè** (**40min**), following the ascent route in reverse.

The vista extends to the Sciliar as Bolzano and the snow-capped Ortles-Cevedale chains beyond.

THE CATINACCIO/ROSENGARTEN LEGEND

A famous legend tells of a kingdom of dwarves ruled by King Laurin who once occupied a world of tunnels and caves filled with fabulous treasures, deep in the mountain's rocky recesses; in contrast, outside was a carpet of flourishing red roses – whence the German name Rosengarten. Laurin lost his heart to beautiful Princess Similda and, when refused her hand in marriage, he kidnapped her by magic. Furious battles ensued, the maiden was rescued and the dwarf king captured. Laurin later escaped and cursed his beloved roses for leading the enemy to his kingdom. He turned them to stone: never again during day or night would they bloom. Luckily, he forgot the in-between times so it is that every evening after sunset the king's red roses appear in their glowing splendour for a few moments prior to nightfall. This is known evocatively in the Ladin language as *Enrosadira* (Alpenglow), and luckily can be enjoyed all over the Dolomites.

WALK 38
Sentiero del Masaré

Start	Passo di Costalunga
Finish	Malga Frommer
Distance	12.2km
Ascent/Descent	670m
Grade	2
Walking time	4hr 20min
Maps	Tabacco n.029 or n.06 scale 1:25,000
Refreshments	Passo di Costalunga, Drei Schupfen, Rifugio Roda di Vael, Rifugio Fronza
Access	A SAD bus from Bolzano runs to Passo di Costalunga 12 months a year, as does one from Malga Frommer back to the intersection just below Passo di Costalunga.

The beautiful Catinaccio group (known to German speakers as the Rosengarten, in memory of a legendary dwarf king whose garden of red roses flourished miraculously on the barren mountain flanks – see Walk 37) is one of the Dolomites' most popular destinations for summer walkers and climbers.

A saunter along the Sentiero del Masaré (Hirzelweg in German) beneath the imposing western rim of the soaring Catinaccio, is simply brilliant, with plenty to admire. Named in memory of the Leipzig publisher Hirzel who envisioned it in 1904, it follows the natural lay of the mountain in the shape of an elongated horizontal layer-cum-ledge.

The walk consists of ascent on a good path, followed by a long scenic tract with several narrow cable-aided stretches where erosion is ongoing. It terminates with a steepish drop back to road level. The walk can also be accessed by way of Rifugio Paolina, thanks to the chairlift that departs downhill from Passo di Costalunga; this cuts around 1hr 30min off the total time.

From Passo di Costalunga (1745m) alongside Pensione Rosengarten, track n.548 initially strikes out N on a

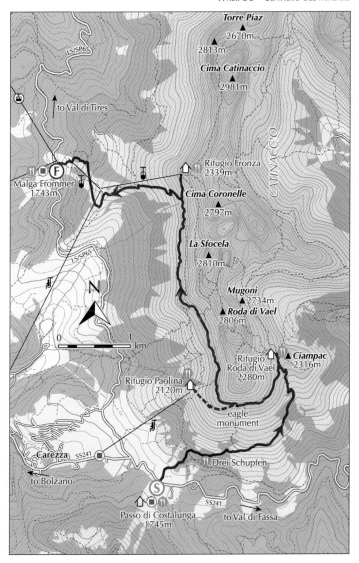

Closer at hand are the Mugoni, once a favourite haunt of witches who threw wild parties, hurling flaming wheels onto the Cigolade crest, the name meaning 'burnt'.

He was a Viennese entrepreneur whose brainchild was the 1909 construction of the 'Great Dolomite Road' linking Bolzano and Cortina, not to mention the stately Grand Hotel Carezza below.

tarmac surface that quickly gives way to dirt. At a 1795m fork (15min), it branches R as a rough lane, steep at times, past chalets and a farm-cum-café **Drei Schupfen**. You traverse light mixed wood brightened with plenty of wildflowers beneath crumbly mountain flanks. Veer N for the zigzag climb through thinning pasture, heading towards rockscape to join upper path n.549. A R turn will take you to **Rifugio Roda di Vael** (2280m, **1hr 30min**) in its scenic saddle looking to the Sella and the Marmolada. ◄ Vast views are also on offer from the neighbouring 2316m hump known as Ciampac.

Backtrack on n.549, and keep strolling SW. This broad stretch is immensely popular – it coasts between 2200–2300m, giving ample opportunities to admire the changing views. The Latemar massif is especially striking.

Where the path rounds the southernmost point of the Masaré, a bronze **eagle monument** (2280m, **20min**) in honour of Theodor Christomannos ◄ stands on a grassy knoll. (It can be accessed from Rifugio Paolina (20min): from the chairlift arrival at Rifugio Paolina (2120m), take well-trodden path n.539, which climbs ESE to join the main route near the eagle monument.)

The landmark bronze eagle monument in honour of Theodor Christomannos

Stick to the upper path, which heads mostly N now towards the massive bulk and sheer 400m face of Roda di Vael. Slightly exposed at times, it crosses fascinating eroded red rock-earth gullies where the Werfen strata have been laid bare to the elements. One ledge section is reassuringly cable aided. Ignore the fork R – n.9 to Passo del Vaiolon. The path eventually drops briefly, and passes another link with Rifugio Paolina.

Keep on n.549 N for the final stretch including a stream crossing beneath the Coronelle. At a junction with a broad lane n.1 (the route down to Malga Frommer), branch R up to the new gondola lift, a short stroll from **Rifugio Fronza** (2339m, **1hr 30min**). ▸

This popular rambling hut occupies a panoramic setting, and is also referred to by its original German name Kölner Hütte (it was built by the Cologne Alpine Club in 1889).

If you do not opt for the mechanised descent to Malga Frommer, retrace your steps on path-lane n.1 dropping decisively past the path junction you arrived at earlier. Near the gondola lift middle station and a chairlift (2000m), track n.15 takes over. Further down it cuts through wood to the lower **lift station** and friendly **Malga Frommer** (1743m, **1hr**), a good place for refreshments, as well as the bus back to Passo di Costalunga. ▸

In the absence of a bus, allow 1hr 40min for the signed walking route running parallel to the road back to Passo di Costalunga.

WALK 39
The Latemar Labyrinth and Lago di Carezza

Start/Finish	Grand Hotel Carezza
Distance	10.8km
Ascent/Descent	400m
Grade	1–2
Walking time	3hr
Maps	Tabacco n.06 or 029 scale 1:25,000
Refreshments	Lago di Carezza
Access	The Grand Hotel and bus stop are 2.5km W of Passo di Costalunga, served by year-round SAD buses between Bolzano and Val di Fassa.
Warning	Rockfalls are not uncommon and sections of the path may be temporarily closed.

The Latemar is an imposing massif that emerges from a thick forest of pines. Its airy crest is a jagged line-up of slender eroded rock spires and towers – petrified dolls according to one imaginative tale. The name probably came from 14th-century Ladin *mora* (or *mara*) for the unusual flows of scree it produces. Beneath the north face of the Latemar, a basin rimmed with pine trees harbours delightful Lago di Carezza. It is 250 metres long and 125 metres wide, with a depth that varies between 5–17m, depending on snowmelt and underground sources. The best period to visit is early summer, when it is more likely to be full.

A well-kept path these days, equipped with red arrows and cairns, the Labyrinth makes for a delightful, leisurely half-day walk, and it is a good first walk in the Dolomites – especially as this loop version also takes in the gorgeous lake. Visitors will notice swathes of open land and tree stumps – the effect of the October 2018 storm Tempesta Vaia. The 'good news' is that the lake is now visible from different viewpoints!

THE LABYRINTH

Tourism discovered this area in the mid-1850s, when ingenious engineers cut a road through the dramatic red porphyry gorge Val d'Ega, creating a link with Bolzano. A Grand Hotel was inaugurated in 1896, rapidly becoming a glamorous summer residence for aristocracy. Foreign visitors included Winston Churchill and Agatha Christie, who set the conclusion to her 1927 thriller *The Big Four* on the Labyrinth route that runs below the Latemar's dramatic northern flanks:

We were hurried through the woods at a break-neck pace, going uphill the whole time. At last we emerged in the open, on the mountain-side, and I saw just in front of us an extraordinary conglomeration of fantastic rocks and boulders. This must be the Felsenlabyrinth of which Harvey had spoken. Soon we were winding in and out of its recesses. The place was like a maze devised by some evil genie.

On the roadside opposite the marvellous old-style Grand Hotel Carezza (1609m) is a path that quickly leads R to the start of a forestry lane L, marked n.13. Not far up ignore both the fork n.10 R (the return route) and a track

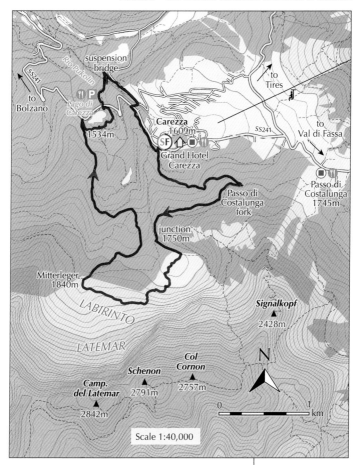

L. The Latemar rears above the trees ahead as you climb easily S then E, through clearings in the pine forest. ▶

Up at a signed **fork** where you are joined by a route from Passo di Costalunga, turn R on n.13 but leave it only metres on for path n.21, R. This is a lovely route SW through the forest with shoulder high plants and

Purple orchids and lilac adenostyles colour the undergrowth.

197

An opening in the wood shows the proximity of the towers and sheer flanks of the Latemar.

Lago di Carezza backed by the Catinaccio

occasionally mud. A short descent brings you to a lane **junction** (1750m, **50min**) where you turn L on n.18. ◄

Not far along, n.20 forks R (SW) to cross a silted basin at the foot of the mountain. It quickly becomes clear why this is known as the Labirinto as guided by red/white waymarks you find yourself weaving in and out of – not to mention beneath – gigantic toppled boulders left by ancient rockslides. The ground has been colonised by thick carpets of mountain avens, while streams of stones

illustrate the interesting mix of light-coloured limestone interspersed with black volcanic fragments.

Some clambering is involved on the way to the 1900m mark below the Latemar's crazily eroded spires (Torri del Latemar), while the spread of the beautiful Catinaccio appears behind you. The path re-enters woodland before traversing dramatic rivers of scree. It emerges at meadows and a huddle of timber huts at **Mitterleger** aka Lega di Mezzo (1840m, **50min**).

Turn R down the wide forestry lane (n.11) for the leisurely descent N. Down near the road is **Lago di Carezza** (1534m, **45min**) and its extraordinary colours, ensconced in the dark green fir forest. Fork sharp R to circle the lake, and take time out at the viewing platform.

LAGO DI CAREZZA

Lago di Carezza (Karersee in German) is renowned for its brilliantly coloured crystal-clear waters, precious jewels buried in its sandy floor according to one legend. A tale stars a graceful nymph who sang at the water's edge. Alas, she attracted a crafty wizard who forged a marvellous rainbow to dazzle her. However the plan went awry, the nymph was saved and the furious wizard smashed the rainbow into smithereens which fell into the lake, the colours melting in the water.

Afterwards go through the tunnel under the road to the toilets, cafés and shops, then head through the **car park**. Keep R over a marvellous **suspension bridge** then take the next fork R (n.6 signed for Paolina). Up at a minor road turn R again and follow the tarmac the short distance to the main road. Here cross over and go L on lane n.10 for the stroll back to the **Grand Hotel Carezza** (**35min**).

WALK 40
Circumnavigating Sassopiatto-Sassolungo

Start/Finish	Passo Sella
Distance	16.5km (11km for exit via Rifugio Demetz)
Ascent/Descent	850m (1150m for exit via Rifugio Demetz)
Grade	2
Walking time	6hr (5hr 30min for exit via Rifugio Demetz)
Map	Tabacco n.05 scale 1:25,000
Refreshments	Passo Sella, Col Rodella, Rifugio Friedrich August, Rifugio Pertini, Rifugio Sassopiatto, (Rifugio Vicenza, Rifugio Demetz), Rifugio Comici
Access	Passo Sella links Val di Fassa with Val Gardena and has summer SAD buses from all directions. A handy alternative access is the cable car from Campitello in Val di Fassa to Col Rodella, near Forcella Rodella. Car parking at Passo Sella is all but unthinkable in summer.

The Sassopiatto-Sassolungo is the attractive centrepiece for this very promising walk, which features a crazy kaleidoscope of amazing Dolomites shifting in focus all around. The opening section was baptised the Friedrich August Weg. Ideated by the last King of Saxony, an expert mountaineer and keen Dolomiter, the beautiful broad pathway dotted with hospitable huts follows ancient shepherds' routes. This stretch can get crowded however the further you go the quieter it gets. Be aware that the surrounds of Passo Sella get incredibly busy in midsummer, and the slopes are popular for picnics, so do make an early start. A variant return is given through the severe inner realms of Sassolungo; marginally more difficult, it concludes with a memorable historic gondola lift ride.

From Passo Sella (2183m) at the rear of the hotel, take path n.557, not far from the gondola lift. It cuts SW across grassy flowered hillsides to link up with a broad dirt track past huts and ski lifts. On the Friedrich August Weg now you'll find yourself climbing steadily past lazing cows to

SASSOPIATTO-SASSOLUNGO

Then come the gigantic masses of the Platt Kofel and Lang Kofel; the first, sliced off, as by the malice of a Titan, at a single blow; the second, an array of splintered spires, ashy-tinted or pale yellow.

Gilbert and Churchill (1864)

Sassopiatto-Sassolungo (Plattkofel-Langkofel in German) or 'flat stone-long stone' are attached at the middle. The former is a 45-degree inclined slab – in aerial photos it resembles a bleached volcanic crater open on one flank – while the latter is a clutch of dramatic rock points, likened to a Gothic cathedral by 18–19th-century topographer JJ Staffler, though according to legend the Bregostane nymphs used to hang out their washing on the spires.

When you stand at Passo Sella and look up at the mountain, it doesn't take much imagination to see the northernmost block as a massive head flanked by a huge hand – the Cinque Dita (five fingers). Legend says they belonged to a thieving giant, punished with burial up to his neck with his hand sticking up and open, to show that it was empty!

Forcella Rodella (2318m, **30min**), just below Rifugio des Alpes and the Col Rodella cable car from Campitello in Val di Fassa (alternative entry). ▶

Heading NW you soon pass **Rifugio Friedrich August** (2298m), named after the king, who is portrayed in a wonderfully carved wooden statue of excellent Val Gardena workmanship. Above is the evocative Cinque Dita formation alongside Forcella Sassolungo, its hut visible.

You soon drop on steps to an earth path which crosses a series of streams below exposed soil layers. ▶ Fallen rocks, gentians and Arolla pines accompany you to cosy **Rifugio Pertini** (2300m), in memory of a popular past president of Italy. Not far along, more exciting views open up ahead, with the Catinaccio and the adjacent Sciliar. Stick with n.557 via a grassy ridge over a summer farm to the base of the vast Sassopiatto slab slope, occupied by the popular and hospitable **Rifugio Sassopiatto** (2300m, **1hr 30min**).

The marvellous views here – to the terraces of the Sella, Marmolada and Gran Vernel – are a good excuse for taking a breather.

If wet, the way can be slippery and even muddy. Overhead are soaring rock pinnacles named after renowned mountaineers Grohmann and Innerkofler.

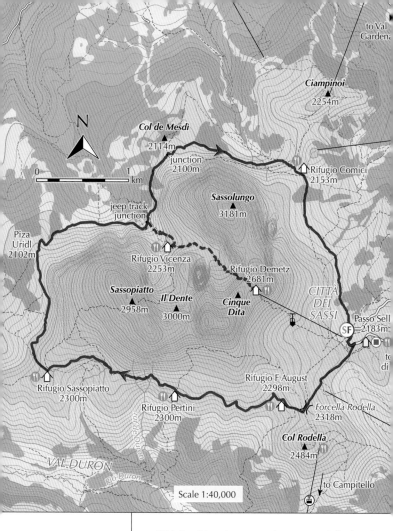

To Val Gardena

Ciampinoi
2254m

Col de Mesdi
2114m

junction
2100m

Rifugio Comici
2153m

Sassolungo
3181m

jeep track
junction

Piza
Uridl
2102m

Rifugio Vicenza
2253m

Rifugio Demetz
2681m

CITTA
DEI
SASSI

Sassopiatto
2958m

Il Dente
3000m

Cinque
Dita

Passo Sell
2183m

SF

to
di

Rifugio Sassopiatto
2300m

Rifugio F August
2298m

Rifugio Pertini
2300m

Forcella Rodella
2318m

Col Rodella
2484m

VALDURON

to Campitello

Scale 1:40,000

With inspiring views over the pasture idyll Alpe di
Siusi, n.527 drops quickly down a dirt track, soon leaving it for a lovely path off to the R (N). Across thickly
flowered hillsides, the route makes a relaxing traverse to
the eroded earth ridge **Piza Uridl** (2102m). Arolla pines

The Cinque Dita above Forcella Sassolungo and Rifugio Demetz. Awesome.

punctuate the ensuing drop to where you ignore a minor turn-off L (for S Cristina). Decidedly E you embark on a steepish climb via scree gullies, heading for the innermost valley, where you emerge on the **jeep track (1hr 30min)** from S Cristina. Fork R (puff, puff) but, unless you opt for the tiring variant via Rifugio Vicenza to Rifugio Demetz and the gondola lift return to Passo Sella, leave the track at the next bend for a path L.

Exit to Passo Sella via Rifugio Demetz and gondola lift (2hr)

Relentless zigzags lead up into the inner realms of the Sassopiatto-Sassolungo, amid blindingly bleached scree and astonishing clumps of Rhaetian poppies. The attractive stone building **Rifugio Vicenza (2253m, 30min)** is well camouflaged in an awesome setting. Although it looks out over Val Gardena, it is very much dominated by the towering, almost suffocating peaks.

The path is a little more difficult from now on, entailing a further 400m in ascent on n.524 up a silent rock gully which harbours snow well into the summer – take extra care. Sheer rock walls and towers dwarf mere walkers en route to **Rifugio Demetz** (2681m, **1hr 30min**) at the narrow opening of Forcella del Sassolungo. Ride the historic gondola lift down to **Passo Sella**. ◀

Main route

Keep almost immediately R to quickly join n.526, a beautiful traverse N before a short uphill stretch to a key **junction** (2100m) close to eroded **Col de Mesdì**. Here, don't be tempted by the upper path R as prone to rockfalls it has tricky sections, but take the slightly lower broader one veering due E on a lovely long traverse at the foot of the awesome northern walls of Sassolungo. ◀ Over scree and through trees it joins wide lane n.528 up to café-restaurant **Rifugio Comici** (2153m, **1hr 45min**). ◀

To complete the circuit, it's a leisurely coast S through woods on n.526. Keep straight ahead at a fork, and up to a ridge junction. Over a style path descends to wind its way through an unearthly landscape of tumbled

Don't be tempted by the scree path below the lift as it is extremely steep and unstable.

If you inadvertently follow the upper path, further around, a scree slope will lead you plunging down to pick up n.526.

The sight of the looming Sella group straight ahead will take your breath away!

The walk's last leg crosses the scattered boulders of the Città dei Sassi at the foot of Sassolungo

boulders, an ancient rockfall dubbed 'Città dei Sassi' (city of stones). You finally emerge at **Passo Sella** (**45min**).

WALK 41
The Sella and Piz Boè

Start/Finish	Passo Pordoi cable-car station
Distance	8km (+2km for alternative to Forcella Pordoi)
Ascent/Descent	560m (+600m for alternative to Forcella Pordoi)
Grade	2–3
Walking time	3hr 15min (+1hr 35min for alternative to Forcella Pordoi)
Maps	Tabacco n.05, 06 or 07 scale 1:25,000
Refreshments	Passo Pordoi, Sass Pordoi, Rifugio Forcella Pordoi, Rifugio Boè, Capanna Fassa
Access	Passo Pordoi has SAD summer buses from Val di Fassa, Val Gardena and Arabba.

The Sella boasts a pyramidal peak, 3152m Piz Boè, of relatively straightforward access to non-climbers – in optimum conditions, usually midsummer or early autumn, and preferably with perfect visibility! The most dramatic walker's summit anywhere in the Dolomites, it is the highest point reached in this guide.

The route described here makes the most of a cable car that takes the sting out of the steep approach from Passo Pordoi, although an alternative on foot is given. Overall, the walk rates as fairly difficult due to the exposed partially aided stretches on the actual summit route. Be aware that the Sella is (justifiably) an extremely popular destination summer long, so September is probably the most suitable month to visit.

THE SELLA

Bound by sheer rock walls like an isolated fortress, the colossal Sella group has massive terraces cleft by awesome gullies that make it an instantly recognisable landmark. Windswept and snowbound at length, the overwhelming impression is of a stone desert, not exactly inviting for walkers at first sight.

Originally a coral reef, it is a treasure trove of fossilised ammonite shells. There is not a tree to be seen. But there is no lack of vegetation thanks to lichens and hardy, brightly-coloured, ground-hugging flowers. Animal life too is surprisingly easy to see – huge flocks of optimistic alpine choughs on the lookout for visitors' scraps, as well as stable populations of sturdy ibex and nimble chamois.

From the cable car on Sass Pordoi, follow the main route description as far as the refuge then retrace your steps (2hr 20min there and back).

A curiosity: it took 580 helicopter trips to transport the material needed to construct this chalet!

The cable car from Passo Pordoi (2239m) whisks you up to **Sass Pordoi** at 2950m before you know it. Perched on this corner of the gigantic Sella, you get stunning views of the Catinaccio, Sciliar and Sassopiatto-Sassolungo, while closer at hand is the stark plateau of the Altopiano delle Meisules and bizarre Piz Ciavazes, a mountain atop a mountain. An easier (Grade 1–2) return walk can be made to Rifugio Boè with minimal height gain and loss. ◀

Once you've taken all that in, make your way past the restaurant, Rifugio Maria, and head NE – with everyone else – for the brief descent on n.627A across bare rock (marked with cairns).This arrives at the narrow opening **Forcella Pordoi** (2829m, **10min**), which shelters a welcoming refuge of the same name. ◀

Passo Pordoi where the walk starts. Sass Pordoi soars above, with its cable-car station.

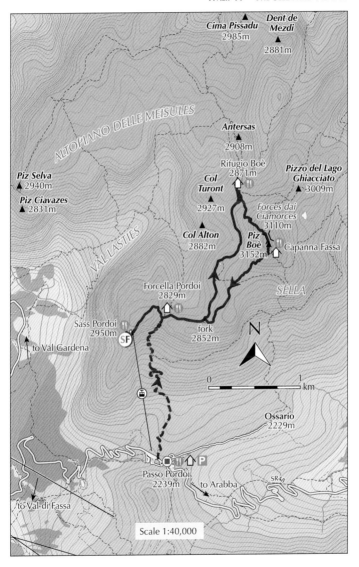

Alternative on foot to Forcella Pordoi (1hr 45min)

From **Passo Pordoi**, path n.627 (also marked Alta Via 2) climbs steadily N over grassy terrain, before zigzagging up scree in view of the dangling cable car. The last leg hugs the cliff, and a cable and flight of steps help with the steep gradient. ◄ After a 600m climb, you clamber out at **Forcella Pordoi**.

Main route

Follow path n.627 due E along a broad natural ledge through a landscape of white-yellowy-grey rock. At the nearby **fork** (2852m, and the return route from Piz Boè), keep L on n.627 to head N across the vast rock upland, over ledges studded with fossilised shells. Follow the cairns, poles and waymarks carefully across the undulating terrain, inevitably spread with well-trodden snow patches, as well as curious red boulders and a pyramid of stones. There are several stretches where reassuring cables can be used. Welcoming state-of-the-art **Rifugio Boè** (2871m, **45min**) stands out on the southern slope of Antersas. ◄

Now gird your loins for the summit attempt. Well-trodden n.638 begins to climb SE, making its way across scree. It heads steeply for a prominent bastion and an aided stretch with steps traversing R which can prove difficult in icy conditions. More steep scree leads to **Forces dai Ciamorces** (3110m). All effort is amply rewarded. Now it's a mere 10min to breathtaking **Piz Boè** (3152m, **1hr 20min**) which hosts a radio mast and cosy wooden hut **Capanna Fassa**, which does a great job serving starving walkers. ◄

From here, all ways lead down. A little easier than the way up, the descent route n.638 follows the broad ridge SW, scrambling down the steep outward corner with some cable aiding and hands-on sections. In good conditions, it is not particularly difficult. Then you traverse a series of rock platforms gradually dropping to the 2852m fork where it's L back to **Forcella Pordoi** (**40min**).

The short ascent path leads back to **Sass Pordoi** and the cable car (**20min**) for the ride back to **Passo Pordoi**. From here, an interesting stroll takes the quiet surfaced lane ENE to the **Ossario** (2229m) aka Sacrario. ◄

Icy snow is common in early summer and autumn.

The original building, erected in 1898 by the Bamberg DÖAV (with building material backpacked up by local porters!), was devastated during WW1. SAT, the Trento CAI branch, rebuilt it and recently made superb extensions.

This is an unbeatable spot with wide-ranging panoramas! Out with the map and compass (or app).

This stark but moving military mausoleum contains the remains of 8000 German and Austrian soldiers from World War 1, and 800 from WW2.

WALK 42
Viel del Pan

Start/Finish	Passo Pordoi/Arabba
Distance	6.5km
Ascent	380m
Descent	150m
Grade	1–2
Walking time	2hr 20min
Maps	Tabacco n.06, 07 or 015 scale 1:25,000
Refreshments	Passo Pordoi, Rifugio Fredarola, Rifugio Viel del Pan, Porta Vescovo
Access	Passo Pordoi has SAD buses from Val di Fassa, Val Gardena and Arabba through summer. Arabba has Dolomiti Bus links year-round.

An age-old trade route, the Viel (or Vial) del Pan runs along the elongated spine of the Padon chain. In the late Middle Ages, it was used by grain smugglers to avoid the heavy taxes imposed by the Venetian Republic, hence the reference to bread (*pan*) in the name. In the late 1800s the lovely path was fixed up by the German Alpine Club and labelled the Bindelweg, after the president of the time.

The Viel del Pan is a highly recommended, straightforward walk that affords unparalleled views of the 'Queen of the Dolomites', the wonderful 3343m Marmolada, which is clad in a shrinking glacier (see Walk 44 for more). The walk concludes with a cable car descent to the resort of Arabba; however, by all means retrace your steps from Rifugio Viel del Pan to Passo Pordoi – allow 2hr.

Alongside Hotel Savoia at Passo Pordoi (2239m), path n.601 (also Alta Via 2) begins a gentle ascent round the outcrop of Sass Beccè past a chapel and romping marmots. Beyond golden carpets of globe flowers, there are beautiful views to the majestic Catinaccio and, very soon, to the Marmolada cradling its sprawling snowfield.

Touching on winter ski lifts, the way curves L past **Rifugio Fredarola** (2400m), set on a lovely scenic platform.

Now the Viel del Pan begins in earnest, a well-worn track just wide enough for the mini tractor used by the hut ahead for transporting supplies. Conglomerate boulders flank the path as it cuts mostly E over slopes thick with an amazing wealth of wild blooms, including black vanilla orchids and pasque flowers. ◄ Not far along, there is a splendid natural podium perfect for 'me and the Marmolada' snapshots. Then around a few more corners stands bustling **Rifugio Viel del Pan** (2432m, **1hr**), the walk's approximate halfway mark. Directly opposite the Gran Vernel peak, it is a great place for a splendidly panoramic lunch – the summer crowds attest to the quality of the cooking.

Set in the grassy flanks above are dark eroded volcanic cusps, reminiscent of Easter Island statues.

Continuing E and becoming a bit quieter now, the Viel del Pan skirts below castle-like Sasso Cappello (also

The Viel del Pan follows path n.601

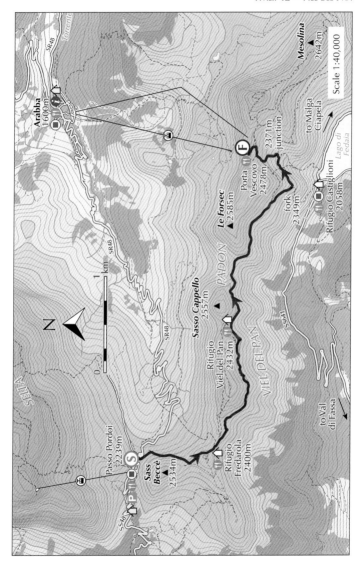

The Viel del Pan

Ahead, beyond Lago di Fedaia and its dam at the foot of the Marmolada, the magnificent Civetta stands out.

known as Sas Ciapel) then touches on two saddles in the crest affording marvellous views to the Sella massif topped by the pyramidal Boè peak. Next come the black lava pinnacles Le Forfesc, reportedly the haunt of ageing prince Vögle delle Velme when in a dark mood! ◄

A good way along, watch out for a **fork** (2349m), where you need to go L (n.601A). After a level stretch NE to huts and a **junction** (2371m), branch sharp L (due N) for a short, steepish climb. This brings you up to a snack bar on the tufaceous Padon ridge at the space-age station of **Porta Vescovo** ('bishop's door'; 2478m, **1hr 20min**). ◄ The cable car takes its time to proceed down the 900m drop to **Arabba** (1600m), giving you ample time to admire the Val Badia Dolomites en route.

An earlier World War 1 cable car ran here to supply Austrian positions along the crest.

THE PADON CHAIN

Running east–west, the Padon is of dark volcanic origin, in stark contrast to the pale shades of the Sella and Marmolada that it separates. Legends and rumours were once rife of an underground realm peopled by subjects doomed never to see the light of day in return for fabulous treasures. The fertile earth, a rich chocolate brown, sustains a remarkable carpet of jewels in the shape of wild flowers and keen eyes will pick out an edelweiss or two among the multi-coloured blooms. It also guarantees rich pasture for the flocks of sheep brought up to graze in the company of timid chamois, all apparently unperturbed by sheer cliff edges devoid of protective fencing.

WALK 43

The Sas de Adam Crest

Start/Finish	Ciampac gondola lift/Pozza di Fassa
Distance	8km
Ascent	350m
Descent	450m
Grade	2
Walking time	3hr (less if upper chairlifts are used)
Map	Tabacco n.06 scale 1:25,000
Refreshments	Ciampac, Col de Valvacin, Baita Cuz
Access	Val di Fassa is served 12 months a year by Trentino Trasporti buses which stop at both the walk start (the Ciampac gondola car near Alba) and finish (Pozza di Fassa).

This wonderful walk follows the exciting Sas de Adam crest, of great geological interest. As lifts are used at both start and finish, it can be completed in a half-day, although it's a pity to rush. You follow straightforward, clearly marked tracks and paths and the only difficulty encountered is on the narrow central section, which, in wet conditions, would be a little slippery and could be dangerous. However, as the main attraction of the route is its great scenic appeal, it wouldn't be worth undertaking it in bad weather in any case!

GEOLOGY OF THE SAS DE ADAM

Way back in geological time, as coral beds and marine debris were being deposited in shallow tropical seas, underwater volcanoes were simultaneously issuing streams of red-hot lava. These broke through the pale surface layers and left a heritage of dark rock. A drawn-out process of hardening, uplifting and erosion produced metamorphic islands in a sea of pale sedimentary dolomite seen today in upper Val di Fassa, the Sas de Adam a perfect example. Geology enthusiasts will be fascinated by minerals such as amethyst, prehnite and heulandite, not to mention fascinating pillow lava, while the vast panoramas and bounty of wild blooms that accompany the path are a boon for everyone.

The area is dotted with pylons for winter ski lifts, but they don't detract from the stunning views over to the unmistakable and magnificent Sass Pordoi and Piz Boè on the Sella.

By gondola car from Alba (1486m) it is a breathtaking trip to **Ciampac** (2160m, **10min**), which is an ample grassy basin bound by dark volcanic formations: Crepa Neigra (suitably named for its colouring of volcanic origin) is northwest, facing the towering Colac (southeast). ◄

Take the broad track (n.644) moving off past café-eateries **Rifugio Ciampac** then up to **Rifugio Tobià del Giagher**. Crossing pasture slopes, you join up (R) with a wide lane to a summer chairlift (a ride to Sella Brunech for the lazy). Now comes a gentle climb SW up the middle of the valley via flowered meadows where livestock graze. At path branches make sure you opt for n.644. The clear saddle **Sella Brunech** (2428m, **1hr**) offers more

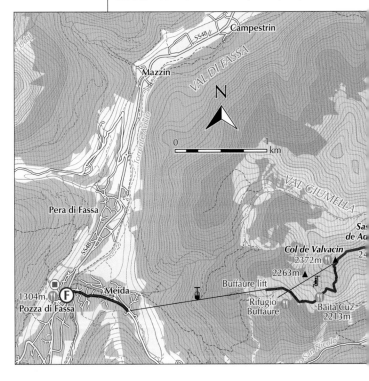

stunning views: Sasso della Croce has now appeared beyond the dark Padon chain, while snowbound Punta Penia on the Marmolada can be seen. Ahead is the extraordinary Catinaccio-Antermoia and the Latemar, backed by the snowbound Ortles.

Ignore the branch for Val Giumella and go L with n.613 now. A brief drop SW crosses slopes thick with thriving alpenrose and bilberry shrubs where marmots might show themselves. Now the narrow path begins to climb the ridge, with dizzy views to Val di San Nicolò below left. The gentle steady ascent with some exposed tracts is brightened by tiny forget-me-nots and cactus-like stonecrop sheltering in rock crannies. ▶ The next

Keen eyes will pick out brick-red crystals of heulandite.

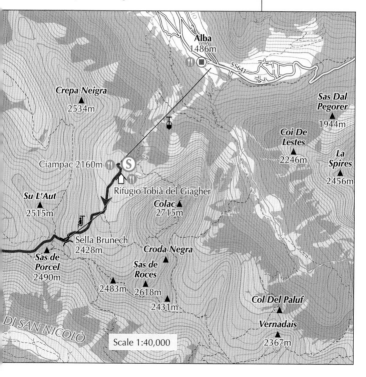

Scale 1:40,000

215

compulsory stop is at **Sas de Adam** (aka Sass de Dama; 2430m, **30min**), for its unbeatable awe-inspiring 360-degree views, which can be enjoyed from giant benches. Out with those binoculars and the PeakFinder app!

After a zigzagging plunge with guiding ropes, you proceed to **Col de Valvacin** (2372m, **20min**) and café Rifugio El Zedron sheltering below. (It's next to a tempting chairlift – by all means indulge in the ride down to Buffaure.)

The path (still n.613) now heads S, facing the Costabella and Monzoni chain, zigzagging down a grassy piste via an old timber hut to cosy eatery **Baita Cuz** (2213m). Keep R (NW, signposted for Bufaure de sot), down the wide stony lane-cum-ski piste. As it goes under the chairlift, don't miss the impressive walls of solidified pillow lava. Immediately after them, a sign for *cabinovia* points you R to the Buffaure gondola lift (2044m, **40min**).

Ciampac backed by the marvellous Sella group

The cabins glide over a pine forest to deposit you at 1325m (**10min**). Head downhill and cross to the left side of the stream. Follow the pedestrian route all the way past a park and take the footbridge R leading out to the main Val di Fassa road and a bus stop (**Pozza di Fassa**, 1304m, **10min**). Here you can catch a bus back to Alba.

The path heads for the Sas de Adam ridge, backed by the Catinaccio

WALK 44
The Marmolada and Punta Serauta

Start/Finish	Malga Ciapela cable car
Distance	2.5km
Ascent/Descent	150m
Grade	2
Walking time	1hr 30min
Maps	Tabacco n.06 or n.015 scale 1:25,000
Refreshments	Malga Ciapela, Serauta cable-car station
Access	Malga Ciapela is on a summer Dolomiti Bus line.

At 3343m, the Marmolada is the 'Queen of the Dolomites', the loftiest mountain in the range. It is renowned for the sprawling albeit rapidly shrinking glacier on its northern face, part of which collapsed dramatically in 2022 causing a tragic loss of lives. The mountain was an arena of hostilities during World War 1 but is now a winter and summer ski playground. This unique walk explores a remarkable high-altitude outcrop riddled with wartime trenches and breathtaking lookouts. It makes use of a cable car (www.funiviemarmolada.com) as far as the second station (Serauta, 2950m), where there is a restaurant and war museum.

The walk itself is quite steep and exposed on the uppermost section, where a little scrambling is required. Keep children within reach at all times. In all, a good half-day will fly by as you wander around, awe-struck. Wrap up warmly, as the air is very chilly up here.

A third dizzy section of the cable car goes as far as the spectacular Punta Rocca lookout at 3250m, recommended for 360-degree views, but stops short of Punta Penia (the crown), which is the exclusive sphere of mountaineers and rightfully out of bounds to tourists.

THE MARMOLADA

Imagine a very thick slice of melon laid upon its side, and you will have a good bird's-eye notion of ... the Marmolata... or else you might think of a vast dead tooth stopped up with snow.

Reginald Farrer's delightful 1913 description.

The 'Queen of the Dolomites' stands 3343m high and 5km long. The earliest known summit attempt was in 1804 when a priest, doctor and lawyer set out to examine the glimmering ice sheet and put an end to superstitious beliefs. However, it was not until 1864 that Punta Penia, the highest elevation, was 'conquered' by Grohmann with the Dimai brothers, his guides.

The age of the glacier is unknown. Rapidly shrinking nowadays, it has lost 80% of its volume over the last century and is destined to disappear in 25/30 years. However, according to legend it was once lush and verdant pasture. One summer evening a lone, old peasant stayed back to rake in her hay, as the weather appeared to be turning bad. Heedless of the admonitions from her companions, who were making for the valley to pay homage to the Virgin and invoke protection for the coming year, she pressed on with her labour. In next to no time she was caught up in a dramatic snow storm – sent as divine punishment! Alas, the weight of the deadly white cloak spelled her end, while the pastures hardened into the icy mass of glacier that sprawls over the slope today.

She has not been alone in her icy tomb. The demarcation line between Italy and the former Hapsburg Empire ran the length of the crest and World War 1 soldiers perished on the treacherous high altitude terrain – the Austrians alone lost 300 men in a single avalanche in December 1916. To shelter their troops, they excavated the ingenious 'City of Ice', an astounding 12km network of tunnels through the glacier's eerie recesses. Survivors told of the uncanny pale blue light, then the spine-chilling creaks and groans of the ice grinding over rock; however they all appreciated the protection it gave them. The retreat of the ice has resulted in poignant war remains coming to light, and a visit to the Serauta war museum is very educational.

Start out from Malga Ciapela (1450m) and ride the first two stages of the cable car as far as the **Serauta station** (2950m). Once you have your breath back, walk downhill NE towards the saddle **Forcella Serauta** (2875m), where you access the remarkably narrow and isolated protuberance of Punta Serauta.

From the map board, follow the arrows for the path to the L, up steps to monuments and a cavern. Keep R along the guiding hand cable and take the first branch L, which leads to a dizzy observation point. Back down on the main path, continue uphill past the *posto comando*

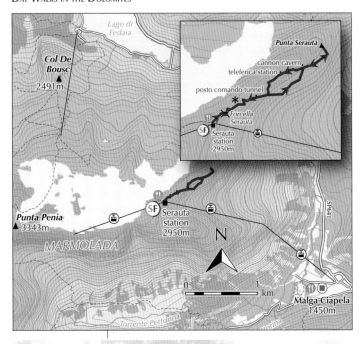

Looking from the walk to the cable-car station on the
Marmolada

tunnel. At the next fork, keep R on the narrow rock path to continue past old shelters and steadily up to a fork near a cavern, which was excavated to house a cannon. Go R again to steps and the cable leading up to the summit crest of **Punta Serauta** (2962m). ▸

Afterwards, taking great care on this partially exposed stretch, return to the fork near the cannon cavern but this time take the R branch. It touches on more shelters, an observatory position and the erstwhile *teleferica* (aerial lift) station. The path then drops to rejoin the lower route, and you turn R back to the monuments and saddle (2875m). It's then a short climb back to the **Serauta station** of the cable car (2950m, **1hr 30min**).

This amazingly spectacular aerial spot overlooks Lago di Fedaia backed by the Padon ridge then the Sella, just for a start. It's hard to know which way to look!

WALK 45
Rifugio Falier in Valle Ombretta

Start/Finish	Malga Ciapela
Distance	12.5km
Ascent/Descent	650m
Grade	1–2
Walking time	3hr 40min
Map	Tabacco n.015 scale 1:25,000
Refreshments	Malga Ciapela, Malga Gran Pian, Malga Ombretta, Rifugio Falier
Access	Malga Ciapela is on the summer Dolomiti Bus line to Lago di Fedaia

This is a delightful, straightforward walk along the foot of the awesome southern wall of the 3343m Marmolada (see Walk 44) following aptly named Valle Ombretta (valley of shade).

It is suitable for family groups, although, in view of the 650m height gain entailed, probably not as a first outing. Frolicking marmots are guaranteed as a large boisterous colony inhabits the middle section of the valley. At Rifugio Falier, walkers with a keen eye may spot the magnificent ibex that graze nonchalantly on the rocky slopes high above the livestock from the summer farms.

VALLE OMBRETTA

It is a mere cup hoisted up upon the side of the Marmolata and at such a height that the south precipice which drops into it, loses much of its expected effect. If the Ombretta had lain as deep as we supposed, then that precipice must have been prodigious ... On the side opposite the Marmolata rise dark snow-patched rocks, and the whole boulder-sprinkled hollow is a perfect specimen of dreariness.

Gilbert and Churchill (1864)

This was their description after an excursion up the valley followed in this walk – go and judge for yourself!

On the southern downhill edge of the small-scale ski resort of Malga Ciapela (1450m), near Albergo Malga Ciapela, take the narrow road (signed n.610) W alongside

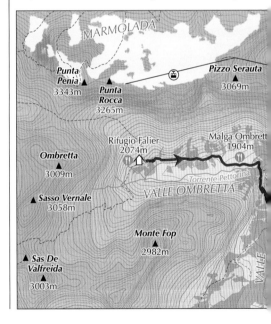

Torrente Pettorina and through a **camping ground**. There are plenty of short cuts on the steady climb through thick forest and flowered pasture clearings. ▶ It's not far to the well-established farm/restaurant **Malga Gran Pian** (1540m, **30min**), which specialises in appetising meals and fresh cheeses.

After a **car park**, the asphalt comes to an end and you cross a bridge where the uphill section starts in earnest. ▶ The dirt track climbs easily, initially S, before you fork R onto a good path NW to climb above the thinning wood. It passes close to a rock face covered with exquisite blooms, including the unusual devil's claw, before reaching an ingenious rock cutting. This leads into the vast grazing reaches of Valle Ombretta, inhabited by sheep and goats under the watchful eye of the shepherd from farm/eatery **Malga Ombretta** (1904m, **1hr**), which is located directly below Pizzo Serauta. Ahead, the valley

The dramatic south wall of the Marmolada rears up NW, while Monte Fop ahead separates the Ombretta and Franzedaz valleys.

The *scorciatoia* short cuts are inadvisable as they're pretty steep. Also, ignore the forks L for Alta Via 2.

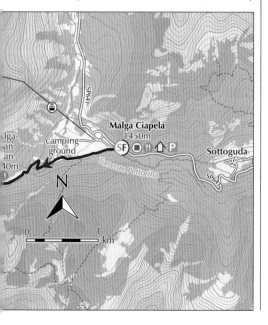

opens up, lined by breathtaking light-coloured walls that provide an inspiring backdrop for a picnic, washed down with delicious fresh water from a hiccupping fountain.

This is the best stretch for observing the playful marmots, who will undoubtedly alert you to their presence with shrill warning cries.

The clear path proceeds W, high above the pasture flat and watercourse. It cuts across lush green hillsides dotted with wild flowers and pines, and punctuated with a gigantic 'H' for the emergency helicopter landing pad. ◀ It's an almost imperceptible ascent to **Rifugio Falier** (2074m, **30min**), an exemplary hut run by a friendly local family who backpacked supplies in for years.

The path climbs easily through the forest en route to Valle Ombretta

The spot affords unforgettable views to the Civetta and Pelmo, which catch the golden rays of the setting sun. The hut was inaugurated in 1911, but the ensuing war left it in ruins and reconstruction had to wait 22 years. Hostilities intervened once again, however, and it was not until 1948 that it could really begin to function properly. It acts as a strategic base for climbers attempting the plethora of challenging routes on the marvellous Marmolada, as testified by the diagrams in the dining room. Directly above the refuge, you can see the metallic building that belongs to the top station of the cable car from Malga Ciapela.

Return to **Malga Ciapela** (**1hr 40min**) the same way you came.

Valle Ombretta opens up with the malga at the foot of the Marmolada's south face

WALK 46
Rifugio Mulaz

Start/Finish	Baita Segantini (alternative start/finish at Passo Rolle)
Distance	12.5km (+6km to and from Passo Rolle on foot)
Ascent/Descent	900m (+200m to and from Passo Rolle on foot)
Grade	2
Walking time	4hr 50min (+1hr 15min to and from Passo Rolle on foot)
Map	Tabacco n.022 scale 1:25,000
Refreshments	Baita Segantini, Rifugio Mulaz
Access	Passo Rolle can be reached by Trentino Trasporti buses from Val di Fassa or San Martino di Castrozza. A summer shuttle bus (*navetta* tel 379 2648349) continues up to Baita Segantini.

Home to chamois, marmots and legendary golden eagles, the northern realms of the spectacular Pale di San Martino group mean soaring pale towers, dizzy high-altitude passes and crazy paths that zigzag up impossible scree slopes above lush pasture valleys. The destination of this walk, Rifugio Mulaz, is superbly located at the head of a dramatic valley crowned with awesome peaks. However getting there involves a lengthy stiff climb and you need to be fit and able to tackle steep terrain with loose rock. Bear in mind that blazing sunshine will make it more testing as there is no shade at all. But all effort is amply rewarded as it's simply spectacular. Lastly, in early summer expect snow cover, especially in the proximity of the refuge.

Alternative start on foot from Passo Rolle (45min)
At a crucifix at Passo Rolle (1980m) dirt track n.710 strikes out N at first. Gently uphill it swings E past **Capanna Cervino** (2082m) where a path cuts straight up the grassy slopes. There are plenty of distractions with alpenrose and masses of globe flowers which flourish in the marshy terrain. The conclusion is **Baita Segantini** (2170m).

Main route

Photogenic café-restaurant **Baita Segantini** (2170m) and its lake come complete with a breathtaking array of light-grey peaks. ▶

Now the dirt track (closed to private traffic here) drops quickly E into the head of Val Venegia, an attractive grazing valley beloved of cows and clad with larches. Around 2000m, path n.710 breaks off R (NE) and touches on the Sorgenti del Travignolo (source of the Travignolo stream). Further along n.710 directs you R for the climb due E, a stiff and relentless slog on loose scree and glaring white rock. Follow the red/white waymarks carefully. ▶

At 2400m you enter a vast upper amphitheatre beneath Campanile di Val Grande and its orange-grey scree flows. Heading NE now, the path struggles up over occasional grass patches where marmots have settled. Ignore a turn-off R for Passo delle Farangole, then you're

Slender Cimon della Pala, the 'Matterhorn of the Dolomites', is dominant, shading the tiny shrinking Travignolo glacier. Another stand-out is Cima della Vezzana.

Despite the stark surrounds, wild flowers such as pink thrift and yellow Rhaetian poppies have taken root.

Rifugio Mulaz and the Focobon peaks

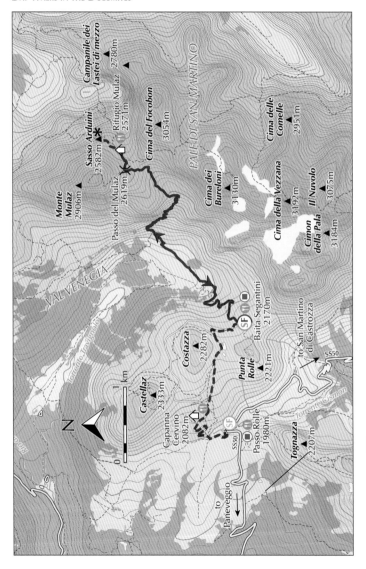

on the final leg to **Passo del Mulaz** (2619m, **2hr 15min**) and the hut's cableway.

This sees you on the verge of an awesome valley with an inspiring view to the hut, the sight of the majestic Civetta beyond. It's an easy stroll down to exemplary **Rifugio Mulaz** (2571m, **15min**), which is powered by solar energy. Constructed in 1907, it faces the magnificent Cima del Focobon, with neighbours Cima di Campidol and Cima Zopel. ▸

The hut's full name is Rifugio Giuseppe Volpi al Mulaz, after the Venetian entrepreneur behind for much of the city's industrial development in the 1920s, and the inaugural Venice film festival in 1932.

Extension to Sasso Arduini (20min return)

From Rifugio Mulaz, path n.753 heads NE (following the AV2 route), ignoring the drop for Falcade. After a saddle, turn off the downhill path then keep R for the narrow passage onto modest **Sasso Arduini** (2582m), a superb viewing platform that is home to exquisite king-of-the-Alps blooms. Return to Rifugio Mulaz when you've had your fill.

Main route

The way back to **Baita Segantini** (**2hr 20min**) is the same as the outward path. Then return to Passo Rolle by shuttle bus or on foot (**30min**).

WALK 47

The Pale di San Martino Altopiano

Start/Finish	Col Verde gondola lift, San Martino di Castrozza
Distance	12km
Ascent/Descent	780m
Grade	2–3
Walking time	5hr 20min
Map	Tabacco n.022 scale 1:25,000
Refreshments	Rifugio Rosetta, Rifugio Pradidali
Access	Trentino Trasporti buses serve San Martino di Castrozza year-round and the Col Verde lift is 5min on foot up the main road.

Starting with rides on two sensational lifts, this exhilarating demanding circuit walk follows a stretch of historic mule track before embarking on an exciting string of averagely exposed rock passages aided by cables, not everyone's cup of tea. It goes without saying that it is unsuitable for inexperienced walkers as well as youngsters. After a drop from Passo del Ball, you climb back up to the wonderful *altopiano*. Two well-run refuges with good facilities are visited.

Warning: Low cloud and mist, fairly common occurrences on the plateau, can transform a straightforward stroll here into a challenging exercise in orienteering, as the undulating rocky terrain has little in the way of recognisable features and it can be tricky getting your bearings. The main paths are marked by pyramidal stone cairns, red and white paint splashes and the occasional signpost. Moreover, walkers in early summer can expect late-lying snow in sheltered valleys.

PALE DI SAN MARTINO GROUP

The multi-faceted Pale di San Martino group dominates the trendy resort of San Martino di Castrozza, which is all but overwhelmed by its sheer flanks. A 'bevy of formidable giants' (DW Freshfield, 1875) encompassing soaring towers, elegant rounded mounts and awesome needles hem in a stone desert: a 20km² *altopiano* lying 2500–2800m above sea level and marked by gibbosity and karstic depressions. Known locally as *buse* (holes), these are relics of the shifting ice sheet that covered everything around 10,000 years ago. Many harbour unassuming lakes, the odd pocket glacier or wind-blown soil where alpine plants have taken root, such as the endemic Moretti's bellflower, yellow Rhaetian poppies and pink thrift, all protected under the Parco Naturale Paneveggio–Pale di San Martino.

Just above San Martino di Castrozza (1470m), the gondola lift (*cabinovia*) glides up to **Col Verde** (1965m), where you transfer to the sensational cable car that terminates on the verge of the breathtaking Pale di San Martino plateau (2609m, **15min**).

Disembark and turn L (NE) down the main path to spick and span **Rifugio Rosetta**, aka Pedrotti, (2578m, **10min**). Beautifully restructured at the hands of the Trento branch of the Alpine Club, it was one of the earliest refuges in the Dolomites, originally constructed in 1889. ▶

Move off R (S) on broad stony mule track n.702/AV2, via **Passo di Val Roda** (2572m), for the drop to skirt the base of Croda di Roda.

MULE TRACK

The brain-child of a Leipzig baron in 1905, under the Hapsburg Empire, the ancient mule track climbs 1000m from San Martino up Val di Roda to the plateau. As the story goes, the workers were paid by the metre rather than on a time basis and, ingeniously, stretched out the path, judging from its interminable zigzags (240 in all!) and all but imperceptible gradient. In another version the gentle gradient was intentional to ensure a smooth ride on horseback for the baron's disabled daughter.

Eventually, 300m lower, you veer L along man-made ledges rounding grassy outcrop Col delle Fede. A level

Badly damaged during WW1 it was rebuilt in 1921, enlarged in 1934, burnt down by German forces in 1943 and eventually brought back to life in 1952 – the usual story!

The Rosetta rears up close to the cable-car station

stretch leads E across a scree valley flanking massive Pala di San Martino. At a **junction** (2270m, **1hr**), you leave the mule track zigzagging crazily downwards, and fork L on n.715. Sticking to the left side of a rubble-filled valley, it narrows and climbs steadily in the shade of Cima di Val di Roda.

A warning sign recommends inexperienced walkers rope up and use karabiners.

◀ This marks the start of a ledge equipped with guiding cable anchored to the rock, which should be tackled with the appropriate care. You edge along narrow passages and clamber hands-on up rock faces. The going is both giddy and very beautiful, before the path reappears for the final leg to the dramatic opening **Passo del**

Ball ▶ (2443m, **1hr**), facing awesome Cima Canali and impressive Sass Maor.

Path n.715 continues in an easy descent E, dodging toppled boulders and scree to **Rifugio Pradidali** (2278m, **20min**). This comfortable building replaces the 1896 hut, which often hosted the King of Belgium on his mountaineering forays.

Leaving behind the hut comforts, drop towards the valley floor and turn L (N) to ascend the desolate upper Val Pradidali. Well-waymarked path n.709 passes silted-up Lago Pradidali followed by a series of scree-strewn terraces, brightened by delightful flowers. There are superb views onto the magnificent line-up of towers and spires – Cima Pradidali and Cima Immink are outstanding. At around 2300m, the route shifts NE, gaining terrace after terrace. Ignore the turn-off R for AV2/Passo delle Lede, as well as that for Passo di Fradusta further up. Keep L (NW) for the final climb to marvellous **Passo Pradidali Basso** (2658m, **1hr 20min**), which overlooks the curious landscape of the plateau. ▶

Path n.709 now bears L (NW). An initial briefly exposed stretch cuts across rock wall, before you begin to make your way over the undulating stone desert. Marvellous Cimon della Pala is ahead, and the refuge is soon visible. Keep a constant eye on waymarking and cairns as you negotiate the tiring ups and downs back to **Rifugio Rosetta** (2578m) then on to the cable car (**1hr**) for the ride back down to **San Martino di Castrozza** (1470m, **15min**).

Named after John Ball, pioneer in Dolomite mountaineering and first president of the Alpine Club in England.

Close at hand is the glittering, shrinking Fradusta glacier, on the north-facing flank of the peak of the same name.

WALK 48
Val Canali and Rifugio Treviso

Start/Finish	Rifugio Cant del Gal, Val Canali
Distance	8km
Ascent/Descent	550m
Grade	2
Walking time	3hr 40min
Map	Tabacco n.022 scale 1:25,000
Refreshments	Rifugio Cant del Gal, Malga Canali, Rifugio Treviso
Access	Fiera di Primiero has year-round Trentino Trasporti bus links. Summer runs go up to Cant del Gal. You can drive as far as the 1300m car park in Val Canali, a saving of 40min.

In the southern reaches of the Pale di San Martino group, Val Canali cuts deep into the rock massif, with awesome sheer walls 1000m high, on either side. Thickly forested, it is alive with animals, including elegant deer and nimble chamois.

This straightforward walk heads for a hospitable hut before traversing mid-height and returning to the valley floor. Rifugio Treviso has creaky wood floors and a cosy dining room, as well as outdoor terraces crowded with climbers of an afternoon, swapping their stories of this prime rock country.

The walk start Cant del Gal means 'rooster's song', a reference to the capercaillie and his courting arena.

From the bus stop at Rifugio Cant del Gal (1180m), take the narrow surfaced road alias n.707 NNE along Val Canali. ◄ There's a small **car park** (1300m, **20min**) near the inviting Malga Canali summer eatery, before the road is barred to traffic. Following the banks of Torrente Canali, a lane continues in the same direction as the surrounds become wilder and more beautiful.

Fork R for the bridge crossing the stream and soon encounter the path from Campigol d'Oltro (the return route). Keep L (NNE) on n.707 to the base of Vallon delle Lede, where you're joined by the AV2 route. Now turn

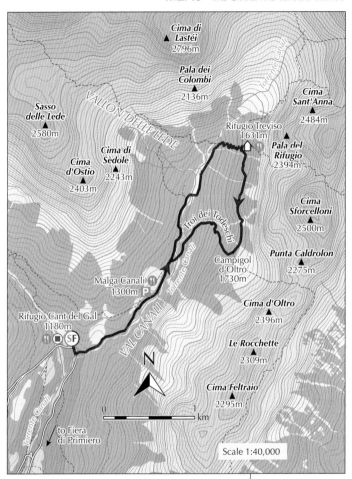

R on a wide uphill path that leads in gentle well-graded curves E through thick conifer forest, never far from waterfalls. The path finally emerges into a small clearing at **Rifugio Treviso** (1631m, **1hr**), a cheerful establishment that serves delicious local meals.

Rifugio Treviso nestling in woodland

Superb views across Val Canali open up, taking in Vallon delle Lede flanked on either side by soaring rock towers.

In common with AV2, walk past the front door of the hut and round the corner, past a wall sundial. Heading S, path n.718 crosses the first of three boulder-choked gullies. In beech and pine forest pretty with purple orchids and adenostyle, it continues mostly on a level. ◄

You finally reach **Campigol d'Oltro** (1730m, **40min**) and a path junction. You now part ways with AV2 and turn R (NW) for a knee-jarring descent in wood thick with flowers and songbirds. This stretch is known as Troi dei Todeschi (the way of the Germans). The 300m descent concludes near the bridge you crossed on the outward leg. Turn L back along the lane in Val Canali to the **car park** (1300m, **1hr 20min**), then on to **Rifugio Cant del Gal** (**20min**).

Lower Val Canali is the site of the Visitor Centre of the Parco Naturale Paneveggio-San Martino at Villa Welsberg, definitely worth a visit for its informative displays.

WALK 49

The Brenta
Dolomites Tour

Start/Finish	Grostè gondola lift/Vallesinella
Distance	13km (8.5km via short cut to Rifugio Casinei)
Ascent	220m (100m via short cut to Rifugio Casinei)
Descent	1140m (1025m via short cut to Rifugio Casinei)
Grade	2
Walking time	5hr 10min (3hr 10min via short cut to Rifugio Casinei)
Map	Tabacco n.053 scale 1:25,000
Refreshments	Passo del Grostè, Rifugio Tuckett e Sella, Rifugio ai Brentei, Rifugio Casinei, Vallesinella
Access	Trentino Trasporti buses provide links with Madonna di Campiglio all year long; the Grostè lift is 2km to its north, also reachable by bus. At walk's end, catch the shuttle bus from Vallesinella to Madonna di Campiglio.

The magnificent straightforward walk described here is both highly recommended and very popular in midsummer. It makes use of a two-stage gondola lift at the start, a superbly scenic way to begin. A long traverse beneath the western flanks of the Brenta ensues, touching on landmark refuges in marvellous spots. It can be shortened by 2hr by exiting at Rifugio Tuckett e Sella.

THE BRENTA DOLOMITES

Through breaks in the forest the glacier-crowned crags of the Cime di Brenta were now seen for the first time, followed on the north by an array of slender obelisks, beaks, and crooked horns, the strangeness of which would, but for a long experience in dolomite vagaries, have made us doubt our eyes.

DW Freshfield (1875)

Located west of the Adige river valley and adjacent to the glaciated metamorphic Adamello range, the Brenta Dolomites are geographically separate from the rest. However, their geological composition and consequently appealing physical morphology, of needle-thin campanile formations and soaring towers, is undeniably Dolomitic. The beautiful chain extends for a length of 40km and width of 12km, and it is blessed with myriad spectacular peaks around the 3000m mark. International mountaineering tourism was launched here in 1864, when John Ball crossed the Bocca di Brenta and wrote it up in the British press. Cima Brenta, at 3151m, is the loftiest peak in the Brenta Dolomites, while Cima Tosa at 3136m comes in a close second. The Brenta range now comes under the Parco Naturale Adamello-Brenta.

This nondescript pass is the key passage to the vast northernmost Brenta group.

The Grostè gondola lift (1646m) means a leisurely trip gliding over stony landscapes to **Passo del Grostè** (2442m, **10min**) and its restaurant. ◄

Path n.316 strikes out SW away from the ski-scarred surrounds into more varied landscapes, on the approach to the spectacular heart of the Brenta. Ahead rears majestic Cima Tosa, its face adorned with hanging glaciers. Walking over stony terrain, you ignore a turn-off for Rifugio Graffer then embark on a series of ups and downs over karstic pavements dotted with long-fallen boulders beneath all manner of spires, towers and needles.

Enjoy freshly baked fruit tarts in this simply glorious location: dominated by Punta Massari and looking up to Bocca del Tuckett with its conical remnant glacier.

Torrione di Vallesinella and the Castelletto Inferiore are outstanding on the final stretch S to well-run twin huts **Rifugio Tuckett e Sella** (2272m, **1hr 30min**). ◄ The older building, inaugurated in 1906 in honour of Quintino Sella (founder of the Italian Alpine Club), was succeeded just a year later by the Berliner Hütte, courtesy of the German Club. At the end of WW1, when the region became Italian, this was renamed in honour of pioneering British mountaineer Tuckett.

Cima
Vagliana
2865m

Pietra
Grande
2935m

Moncuc
2360m

Monte
Spinale
2103m

N

0   1
_____ km

Rifugio Graffer

Le
Crosette
2406m

Passo del
Grostè
2442m

lesinella
513m

Vallesinella
Alta

Sarca di Vallesinella

BRENTA GROUP

Rifugio Casinei
1826m

Torrione di
Vallesinella
2462m

Cima
Grostè
2897m

Campanile
dei Camosci
2920m

Castelletto
Inferiore
2601m

Valle del Fridolin
junction
2043m

Rifugio Tuckett e Sella
2272m

Cima Falkner
2990m

Cima
Sella
2917m

Punta
Massari
2841m

Punte di
Campiglio
2969m

Cima Mandron
3040m

Cima
Brenta
3151m

Rifugio ai Brentei
2187m

Cima degli Armi
2951m

Campanile
Alto
2923m

Crozzon
di Brenta
3130m

Short cut to Rifugio Casinei (1hr)

If time is tight or the weather is not looking good, by all means turn down path n.317 for the direct route to **Rifugio Casinei** (1826m), where you pick up the main route.

Main route

Now path n.328 climbs W, threading its way through a labyrinth of gigantic boulders that dwarf walkers. ◄ A gradual descent through low mountain pines leads to grassy and flower-studded Sella del Fridolin (2143m). Soon the path traverses slippery, sloping rock slabs run through with karstic channelling to the **Valle del Fridolin junction** (2043m, **45min**).

Here you veer L (S) joining n.318 from Rifugio Casinei, entering Val Brenta on a mostly level stretch as the Sentiero Bogani. Ahead, a broad ledge is traversed with the aid of cables. This is followed by a shallow gorge complete with Madonna shrine, then a short rock tunnel. A panoramic climb leads into the narrowing valley, beneath the western walls of Punte di Campiglio. The refuge and chapel soon come into sight under the soaring bulk of Crozzon di Brenta and Cima Tosa, their summits clutching at pockets of snow and ice – remnant hanging

You are afforded bird's eye views onto a vast river of pebbles and gravel borne by glacier meltwater. Obstructed by a rockslide, water flows underground to emerge at waterfalls.

The stunning setting of Rifugio ai Brentei

glaciers. ▶ Wander on to **Rifugio ai Brentei** (2187m, **1hr**), a bustling old-style establishment previously run by Bruno Detassis, a foremost mountaineer who opened up over 100 climbing routes between the 1930s and 1960s.

For the return route, backtrack to the **Valle del Fridolin junction** and continue on n.318 straight ahead in steady descent through woodland to **Rifugio Casinei** (1826m, **1hr 15min**).

Now head NW valleywards on the zigzags of n.317 in shady woods and through grazing land to **Vallesinella** (1513m, **30min**), its café-restaurants and huge car park. Here you can collapse into a bus for the 4.5km back to Madonna di Campiglio.

An arrow indicates a brief detour down R for *acqua* (fresh spring water).

WALK 50
Val d'Ambiez

Start/Finish	Rifugio al Cacciatore (alternative start/finish at Baesa)
Distance	5.7km (17.7km without the jeep taxi)
Ascent/Descent	600m (1550m without the jeep taxi)
Grade	1–2
Walking time	2hr 20min (6hr 30min without the jeep taxi)
Map	Tabacco n.053 scale 1:25,000
Refreshments	Baesa, Rifugio Al Cacciatore, Rifugio Agostini
Access	Baesa and its car park are 3km from San Lorenzo, which has Trentino Trasporti buses. Throughout the summer a jeep taxi acts as a shuttle from Baesa up to Rifugio Al Cacciatore; on request they can pick up passengers at San Lorenzo Tel 333 5909327, www.taximargonari.com.

Fascinating Val d'Ambiez runs for 12km through the southern Brenta Dolomites, and attracts fewer visitors than the more accessible central section (see Walk 49).

No particular difficulty is entailed in the walk, though if you set out on foot from Baesa, do remember it means a hefty 1550m height gain and loss. There are two hospitable huts suitable for lunch.

VAL D'AMBIEZ

A first impression is of a deep river-cut cleft between steep cliffs, while the upper part has retained more ancient features with an ample cirque amphitheatre, moulded by long-gone glaciers. This is surmounted by an awesome crown of typically spectacular Dolomite peaks. Other delights include the *cimitero dei fossili*, an intriguing fossil area, along with marvellous wildflowers and wildlife – birds of prey, herds of chamois, mouflon and deer; binoculars are a must. Farming was long practised here and livestock still graze – Ambiez is believed to come from the Celtic for 'good pasture'.

The valley is pretty hemmed-in here, with no hint of the glories ahead!

The surrounding wood is mostly beech.

The refuge is named for hunters and the chapel is dedicated to Sant'Ubaldo, their patron. Hunting for culling is allowed, under the strict control of the Parco Naturale Adamello-Brenta.

Alternative on foot from Baesa

From Baesa (850m) you follow the rough road (closed to unauthorised traffic) uphill for 6km in total. About 1km uphill, at **Pont de le Scale** (915m), either take the path via the right-hand bank of Torrente d'Ambiez or stick to the road, which crosses to the L side. There's little difference time-wise. ◄ About 30min further along the path, you cross the watercourse and pass **Malga Laon** (1110m) to rejoin the road, which is equipped with concrete runners. ◄

Pretty cascades precede **Pont de Broca** (1304m) and the start of a canyon where the road has been hewn out of the rock. The valley finally starts to widen and you glimpse the towers ahead. At a further bridge, **Pont de Paride** (1547m), the two magnificent Cima di Ceda peaks come into view. The road soon becomes a series of steep ramps that bear L up to pasture clearings. A final effort brings you out on the verge of the vast high-level amphitheatre surrounded by sheer rock walls and a semi-circle of soaring peaks. Close at hand is **Rifugio Al Cacciatore** (1820m, **2hr 30min**), for a well-deserved breather. ◄

Main route

From **Rifugio Al Cacciatore** (1820m) take path n.325 (Sentiero Dallago), which branches L (NW) off the jeep track through bushy low heather, alpenrose and dwarf mountain pines. About 5min on, as the path starts veering

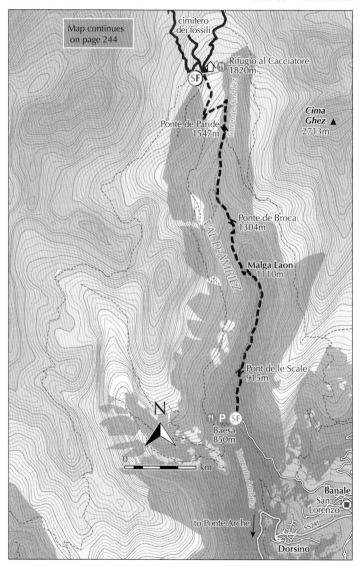

Map continues
on page 244

cimitero
dei fossili

Rifugio al Cacciatore
1820m

SF

Ponte de Paride
1547m

Torrente Ambiez

*Cima
Ghez* ▲
2713m

Ponte de Broca
1304m

VAL D'AMBIEZ

Malga Laon
1110m

Pont de le Scale
915m

N

0   1
km

P   SF

Baesa
850m

Torrente Ambiez

to Ponte Arche ↓

Banale
San
Lorenzo

SS241

Dorsino

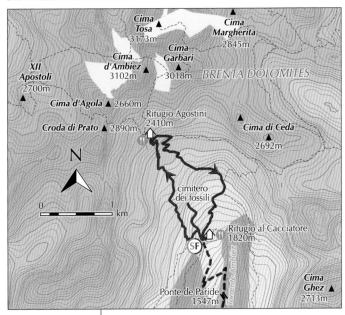

L (S), leave it momentarily for a 30min detour. Take the faint trail that climbs NW towards a terrace.

Continuing past a spring and over horizontal rock strata towards the base of a second terrace, you come into the **cimitero dei fossili** (cemetery of fossils). This is a very interesting karstic zone with parallel ripple-edged decorations (where surface water has sliced through the limestone), the pale slabs embedded with massive fossilised bivalves – Megalodont shells. Once believed to be the hoofprints of the devil, they date back around 200 million years. The rock crannies where precious rock debris and soil have collected have been colonised by mountain avens and even velvety edelweiss. Return to the main path the same way.

Path n.325 resumes its northerly direction across more fissured terrain, with an ever-improving panorama of the cirque and its old moraine ridges, now colonised

The chapel near Rifugio Agostini is set on a belvedere that looks as far as Lake Garda

by vegetation. The path joins the jeep track for the last leg to the marvellous position at the foot of Cima d'Ambiez occupied by **Rifugio Agostini** (2410m, **1hr 30min**), which appears to have been constructed purposefully adjacent to two impressive fallen rocks, which double as a practice wall for climbers. ▶ The chapel on a nearby belvedere provides long-reaching views to Lake Garda and Monte Baldo. There's no lack of picnic spots in the vicinity, and you'll be kept company by inquisitive alpine choughs.

Take the jeep track for the 4km descent. It meanders pleasantly down via ample grazing basins and passes a summer farm a short way before **Rifugio Al Cacciatore** (1820m, **50min**). On foot to Baesa allow 1hr 40min.

Much to the astonishment of the occupants at dawn on 18 July 1957, the two blocks first appeared amid an almighty crash, miraculously coming to a halt just metres away!

APPENDIX A
Useful contacts

Tourist information

The Italian Tourist Board (www.italia.it) has offices all over the world and inspiring websites crammed with all manner of info for intending travellers.

Contact details for tourist offices in the Dolomites follow; they can provide full details of local accommodation options, weather forecasts and transport. To call Italy from abroad use the country code +39 and include the '0' when dialling a landline. Numbers starting with '3' are mobiles.

Alba di Canazei
tel 0462 609550 www.fassa.com

Alleghe
tel 0437 523333 www.dolomiti.org

Alpe di Siusi
tel 0471 709600 www.seiseralm.it

Arabba
tel 0436 79130 www.arabba.it

Belluno
tel 334 2813222
www.adorable.belluno.it

Braies
tel 0474 748660 www.braies.org

Canazei
tel 0462 609601 www.fassa.com

Colfosco
tel 0471 836145 www.altabadia.org

Cortina d'Ampezzo
tel 0436 869086
www.dolomiti.org/it/cortina

Corvara
tel 0471 836176 www.altabadia.org

Dobbiaco
tel 0474 972132 www.dobbiaco.bz

Falcade
tel 0437 599062 www.dolomiti.org

Feltre
tel 0439 2540 www.visitfeltre.info

Fiè
tel 0471 725047 www.seiseralm.it

Fiera di Primiero
tel 0439 62407 www.sanmartino.com

Forno di Zoldo
tel 0437 787349 www.valdizoldo.net

Funes
tel 0472 840180 www.villnoess.com

La Villa
tel 0471 847037 www.altabadia.org

Madonna di Campiglio
tel 0465 447501
www.campigliodolomiti.it

Misurina
tel 0435 39016
https://auronzomisurina.it

Nova Levante
tel 0471 619500 https://eggental.com

Ortisei
tel 0471 777600 www.valgardena.it

Pedraces
tel 0471 839695 www.altabadia.org

Pieve di Cadore
tel 0435 500257www.dolomiti.org

Pozza di Fassa
tel 0462 609670 www.fassa.com

San Candido
tel 0474 913149 www.tre-cime.info

San Cassiano
tel 0471 849422 www.altabadia.org

San Martino di Castrozza
tel 0439 768867 www.sanmartino.com

San Martino in Badia
tel 0474 523175 www.sanmartin.it

Santa Cristina
tel 0471 777800 www.valgardena.it

Selva
tel 0471 777900 www.valgardena.it

Sesto
tel 0474 710310 www.tre-cime.info

Tires
tel 0471 642127 www.seiseralm.it

Vigo di Fassa
tel 0462 609700 www.fassa.com

Villabassa
tel 0474 745136 www.tre-cime.info

Transport
ATVO
www.atvo.it
(Venice–Marco Polo airport–Cortina)

Autostradale
www.autostradale.it (Milano to Cortina,
Val di Fassa, Madonna di Campiglio)

Brusutti
tel 041 5415488
www.brusutti.com (Venice to Caprile,
San Martino di Castrozza and Canazei)

Cortina Express
tel 0436 867350 www.cortinaexpress.
it (Bologna, Mestre and Venice Marco
Polo Airport to Cortina, Val Badia and
Val Pusteria)

Dolomiti Bus
tel 0437 941237 www.dolomitibus.it
(most of the Veneto)

Flixbus
www.flixbus.it
(Mestre to Cortina, Bolzano and Trento)

SAD
tel 0471 220880 www.sii.bz.it (all the
Südtirol)

Trenitalia (trains)
tel 898021 www.trenitalia.com

Trentino Trasporti
tel 0461 821000 www.ttesercizio.it (all
the Trentino)

APPENDIX B
Rifugi

Rifugio Agostini
tel 0465 734138
www.rifugioagostini.com

Rifugio Auronzo
tel 0435 39002
www.rifugioauronzo.it

Rifugio Averau
tel 0436 4660
https://www.rifugioaverau.it

Rifugio Biella
tel 0436 866991
www.rifugiobiella.it

Rifugio Boè
tel 0471 847303
www.rifugioboe.it

Rifugio Bolzano
tel 0471 612024
www.schlernhaus.it

Rifugio Bosi
tel 0435 39034 https://
rifugiobosimontepiana.business.site

Rifugio ai Brentei
tel 0465 441244
www.rifugiobrentei.it

Rifugio Buffaure
tel 339 5951401
www.rifugiobuffaure.com

Rifugio Al Cacciatore
tel 0465 734141
www.rifugiocacciatore.com

Rifugio Capanna Trieste
tel 0437 660122
www.rifugiocapannatrieste.it

Rifugio Casinei
tel 0465 442708

Capanna Cervino
tel 340 0747643
www.capannacervino.it

Rifugio Ciampediè
tel 0462 764432 www.
rifugiociampedie.com

Rifugio Cinque Torri
tel 0436 2902
www.rifugio5torri.it

Rifugio Coldai
tel 0437 789160
www.rifugiocoldai.com

Rifugio Col Gallina
tel 0436 2939
https://rifugiocolgallina.com

Rifugio Demetz
tel 0471 795050
www.tonidemetz.it

Dibaita Puflatsch Hütt
tel 0471 729090
www.dibaita-puflatschhuette.com

Rifugio Dibona
tel 0436 860294
https://rifugiodibona.business.site

Rifugio Falier
tel 0437 722005
http://rifugiofalier.it

Capanna Fassa
tel 0462 601723
www.rifugiocapannapizfassa.com

Malga Federa
tel 324 9249678
www.malgafedera.eu

Rifugio Fodara Vedla
tel 348 8537471
www.fodara.it

Rifugio Fonda Savio
tel 0435 39036
www.fonda-savio.it

Rifugio Fondo Valle
tel 0474 710606
www.talschlusshuette.com

Rifugio Forcella Pordoi
tel 368 3557505
www.rifugioforcellapordoi.com

Rifugio Fredarola
tel 0462 602072
www.fredarola.it

Rifugio Friedrich August
tel 377 3877567
www.friedrichaugust.it

Rifugio Fronza alle Coronelle
tel 0471 612033
www.rifugiofronza.com

Rifugio Galassi
tel 340 1214300
www.rifugiogalassi.it

Rifugio Gardeccia
tel 0462 763152
www.gardeccia.it

Rifugio Genova
tel 0472 670072
www.schlueterhuette.com

Malga Glatsch
tel 0472 670978
www.glatschalm.com

Rifugio Lagazuoi
tel 0436 867303
www.rifugiolagazuoi.com

Rifugio Lavaredo
tel 349 6028675
www.rifugiolavaredo.com

Rifugio Locatelli
tel 0474 972002
www.dreizinnenhuette.com

Rifugio Malga Brogles
tel 338 4600101

Rifugio Malga Ra Stua
tel 0436 5753
www.malgarastua.com

Rifugio Mulaz
tel 0437 599420

Rifugio Nuvolau
tel 0436 867938
https://rifugionuvolau.it

Rifugio Ospitale
tel 0436 4585
www.ristoranteospitale.com

Rifugio Padova
tel 0435 72488
www.rifugiopadova.it

Rifugio Palmieri
tel 0436 862085
www.crodadalago.it

Rifugio Passo Principe
tel 339 4327101
www.rifugiopassoprincipe.com

Rifugio Pedrotti alla Rosetta
tel 0439 68308
www.rifugiorosetta.it

Rifugio Pertini
tel 328 8651993
www.rifugiopertini.com

Rifugio Pian di Cengia
tel 337 451517
www.rifugiopiandicengia.it

Rifugio Pradidali
tel 0439 64180
www.rifugiopradidali.com

Malga Pramper
tel 329 7862899

Rifugio Pramperet
tel 0437 1956153
www.rifugiosommarivaalpramperet.it

Rifugio Pratopiazza
tel 0474 748650
www.plaetzwiese.com

Rifugio Preuss
tel 368 7884968
www.rifugiopaulpreuss.com

Rifugio Puez
tel 0471 1727939
www.rifugiopuez.it

Rifugio Re Alberto
tel 334 7246698
www.rifugiorealberto.com

Baita Resciesa
tel 0471 796174
www.resciesa.com

Rifugio Resciesa
tel 328 3345986
www.rifugioresciesa.com

Rifugio Roda di Vael
tel 0462 764450
www.rodadivael.it

Rifugio San Marco
tel 0436 9444
www.rifugiosanmarco.com

Ospizio Santa Croce
tel 0471 839874
www.lacrusc.com

Rifugio Sassopiatto
tel 0462 601721
www.plattkofel.com

Rifugio Scoiattoli
tel 0436 867939
www.rifugioscoiattoli.it

Rifugio Scotter
tel 347 8314236
www.rifugioscotter.it

Rifugio Sennes
tel 0474 646355
www.sennes.com

Rifugio Tissi
tel 0437 721644
www.rifugiotissi.com

Rifugio Tita Barba
tel 0435 32902

Rifugio Tobià del Giagher
tel 0462 602385

Rifugio Tre Scarperi
tel 0474 966610
www.drei-schuster-huette.com

Rifugio Treviso
tel 0439 62311
www.rifugiotreviso.it

Rifugio Tuckett e Sella
tel 0465 441226
www.rifugio-tuckett.it

Rifugio Vaiolet
tel 0462 763292
www.rifugiovajolet.com

Rifugio Vallandro
tel 0474 972505
www.vallandro.it

Rifugio Vallesinella
tel 0465 442883
www.vallesinella.it

Rifugio Valparola
tel 0436 866556
rifugiovalparola@gmail.com

Rifugio Vandelli
tel 0435 39015
www.rifugiovandelli.it

Rifugio Vazzoler
tel 0437 6600038
www.rifugiovazzoler.com

Rifugio Venezia
tel 0436 9684
www.rifugiovenezia.it

Rifugio Viel del Pan
tel 339 3865241
www.rifugiovieldalpan.com

Rifugio Zsigmondy-Comici
tel 0474 710358
www.zsigmondyhuette.com

APPENDIX C
Italian–German–English glossary

Italian	German	English
acqua potabile	Trinkwasser	drinkable water
acqua non potabile	Kein Trinkwasser	non-drinkable water
agriturismo	Jausenstation	farm that serves meals
aiuto!	Hilfe!	help!
altipiano, altopiano	Hochebene	high-level plateau
aperto/chiuso	geöffnet/ geschlossen	open/closed
autostrada	Autobahn	motorway subject to toll
bivacco	Biwak	unmanned hut for mountaineers
cabinovia, telecabina	Umlaufbahn	gondola lift
campanile	Turmspitze	rock tower, spire
capitello	Wegkreuz	shrine
cascata	Wasserfall	waterfall
casera, malga	Alm	hut or dairy farm
caserma	Kaserne	barracks
castello	Schloss	castle
cengia	Band	ledge
cima	Gipfel	mountain peak
croce	Kreuz	cross
destra/sinistra	rechts/links	right/left
diga	Staumauer	dam
fermata	Haltestelle	bus stop
fiume	Fluß	river
forcella	Scharte	mountain pass for walkers
funicolare	Standseilbahn	funicular railway
funivia	Seilbahn	cable car
galleria	Tunnel	tunnel
ghiacciaio	Gletscher	glacier
giro	Rundgang	circuit
innesto sentiero...	Pfad Graft	joins path...
locanda	Gasthof	guesthouse

Italian	German	English
navetta	Pendelverkehr	shuttle bus
nevaio	Firnfeld	firn, snow field
ometto	Steinmann	cairn
orario	Fahrplan	timetable or opening hours
ospizio	Hospiz	hospice
panificio, fornaio	Bäckerei	bakery
pericolo	Gefahr	danger
piz	Spitze	peak
ponte	Brücke	bridge
previsioni del tempo	Wettervorhersage	weather forecast
rifugio	Hütte	manned mountain hut with food/accommodation
rio	Bach	stream
ruderi	Ruinen	ruins
scorciatoia	Abkürzung	short cut
seggiovia	Sessellift	chairlift
sentiero	Weg, Steig	path
sentiero attrezzato	Gesicherter Wandersteig	aided path
sopra	ober	upper/above
sorgente	Quelle	spring
sotto	unter	lower/below
stazione ferroviaria	Bahnhof	railway station
teleferica	Seilschwebebahn	mechanised goods cableway
torre	Turm	tower
torrente	Wildbach	mountain stream
val, valle	Tal	valley
vedretta	Hängegletscher	hanging glacier
vetta	Gipfel	peak
via ferrata	Klettersteig	aided climbing route

APPENDIX D
Further Reading

Available in libraries, rare book dealers and on the web, inspirational pioneering travel accounts from the mid-1800s and early 1900s make for entertaining reading.

The first ground-breaking work was *The Dolomite Mountains: Excursions through Tyrol, Carinthia, Carniola, and Friuli* by Josiah Gilbert and GC Churchill (1864) followed by John Ball's 1868 *Guide to the Eastern Alps* which says lovely things about the Dolomites.

However one of the best reads is Amelia Edwards' 1873 *Untrodden Peaks and Unfrequented Valleys: A Midsummer Ramble in the Dolomites*. Renowned mountaineer Douglas W Freshfield's *Italian Alps: Sketches in the Mountains of Ticino, Lombardy, the Trentino, and Venetia* (1875) is especially poetic and Reginald Farrer's *The Dolomites* (1913) is another good one.

An inspired black and white film from 1931, *Berge in Flammen* (*The Doomed Battalion*) by Luis Trenker, was made in the Cortina valley and around the Lagazuoi. It narrates the terrible human experiences in the war of mines, in dramatic contrast to the lasting bond of friendship.

Fascinating lighter material can be found in the legends painstakingly gathered in the Dolomite valleys in the late 1800s by Karl Felix Wolff and originally published in the 1930s. An English version is *The Dolomites and their legends*.

Wild flower enthusiasts will appreciate the Cicerone pocket guide *Alpine Flowers* (2019) not to mention the detail and beautiful art work in Christopher Grey-Wilson and Marjorie Blamey's *Alpine Flowers of Britain and Europe* (1995), alas long out of print.

Guidebooks to other routes in the Dolomites
Alta Via 1 – Trekking in the Dolomites by Gillian Price (Cicerone, 2022)
Alta Via 2 + Alte Vie 3–6 in outline – Trekking in the Dolomites by Gillian Price (Cicerone, 2022)
Walking in the Dolomites – 25 Multi-day routes in Italy's Dolomites by Gillian Price (Cicerone, 3rd edition, 2022 reprint with updates)

DOWNLOAD THE ROUTES
IN GPX FORMAT

All the routes in this guide are available for download from:

www.cicerone.co.uk/1121/GPX

as standard format GPX files. You should be able to load them into most online GPX systems and mobile devices, whether GPS or smartphone. You may need to convert the file into your preferred format using a conversion programme such as gpsvisualizer.com or one of the many other such websites and programmes.

When you follow this link, you will be asked for your email address and where you purchased the guidebook, and have the option to subscribe to the Cicerone e-newsletter.

www.cicerone.co.uk

CICERONE

**Trust Cicerone to guide your next adventure,
wherever it may be around the world...**

Discover guides for hiking, mountain walking, backpacking,
trekking, trail running, cycling and mountain biking, ski touring,
climbing and scrambling in Britain, Europe and worldwide.

Connect with Cicerone online and find inspiration.

- buy books and ebooks
- articles, advice and trip reports
- GPX files and updates
- regular newsletter

cicerone.co.uk